Schaumburg Township
District Library

schaumburglibrary.org

Renewals: (847) 923-3158

Gennaro's
PASTA PERFECTO!

*To Antonio, whose day would not be complete
without a steaming plate of pasta!*

Gennaro's

PASTA PERFECTO!

The essential collection of fresh and dried pasta dishes

WITHDRAWN

Gennaro Contaldo

with photography by
David Loftus

Interlink Books

An imprint of Interlink Publishing Group, Inc.
Northampton, Massachusetts

First published in 2020 by
INTERLINK BOOKS
An imprint of Interlink Publishing Group, Inc.
46 Crosby Street, Northampton, MA 01060
www.interlinkbooks.com

Copyright © Pavilion Books Company Ltd. 2020
Text copyright © Gennaro Contaldo 2020
American edition copyright © Interlink Publishing
   Group, Inc. 2020

All rights reserved. No part of this publication may be
reproduced, stored in a retrieval system, or transmitted in
any form or by any means electronic, mechanical,
photocopying, recording or otherwise, without the prior
written permission of the copyright owner.

Library of Congress Cataloging-in-Publication
Data available
ISBN: 978-1-62371-926-5

10 9 8 7 6 5 4 3 2 1

To request our 48-page, full-color catalog, please call us
toll free at 1-800-238-LINK, visit our website at
www.interlinkbooks.com, or send us an e-mail at:
info@interlinkbooks.com.

CONTENTS

Pasta Perfecto

PASTA PERFECTO

I am so excited to be writing a whole book on my favorite food—pasta!

In Italy, pasta is more than just a food—it is a tradition and a way of life, with a long history. In most Italian homes, no meal is complete without a plate of pasta, no matter how it is enjoyed—whether dried, fresh, filled, baked, or served in a soup.

There are many arguments about how pasta first came to Italy, and one is the popular myth that it was brought back by Marco Polo from a trip to China. However, historic evidence shows that *macaroni* and *spaghetti* existed in Italy long before this time and that a pasta known as *lagane* was around in Roman times. *Lagane* was baked rather than boiled, which is probably how our modern-day *lasagne* came to be.

Pasta, as we know it today, started out in the housewives' kitchens of southern Italy, made from the basic ingredients of flour and water. Italy's climate is ideal for cultivating durum wheat, and this is what makes the all-important flour for making pasta. Gradually, it spread throughout the country until it became the beloved staple it is today.

The method of drying pasta was introduced as early as the 1300s, which meant that it could be taken on sea voyages, where its long shelf-life made it the ideal foodstuff. Pasta drying in the streets of Naples in the late 1800s was not an uncommon sight—long strands of pasta would be left out in the hot sun hanging on cane poles resembling washing lines. During my childhood, my home village of Minori had a flour mill and a small pasta factory, and I have vague recollections of the pasta drying in the sun. It would then be packaged in locally manufactured bright blue paper and sold. Over time, drying processes have changed—the traditional methods were updated and technology has taken over. Much larger factories now produce pasta all over Italy, creating a huge and important industry. Probably the largest and most-loved factories producing excellent pasta are in Gragnano, a town not far from Naples.

Whenever Italians emigrated, wherever it was in the world, they brought their beloved pasta with them. This is probably why it became such a globally loved food. Pasta is quick, simple, and versatile. Recipes can range from the speediest, simplest tomato or pesto sauce tossed through some *spaghetti*, to more elaborate and rich baked dishes, or slow-cooked ragù sauces. That's the beauty of pasta—you can make it to suit any occasion and budget, and everyone loves it. Pasta can be made simply with flour and water, or with eggs as it is in northern Italy; it can also be made with wholewheat flour. These days, gluten-free pasta is becoming increasingly popular, with varieties made with lentil and chickpea (gram) flours.

Pasta is very much part of the Mediterranean diet and, if eaten in the right quantity with a good homemade sauce, it is very beneficial to our health. It is an excellent carbohydrate, releasing energy slowly, is cholesterol-free, and has a low glycemic index score, ideal for diabetics. Apart from its nutritional value, pasta also contains serotonin, a substance associated with feelings of peace and contentment.

There is no limit to the joys of pasta and I can quite happily enjoy it every day, cooked in a different way, safe in the knowledge that I am eating a good, nutritional, and balanced diet. I have divided this book into chapters about dried pasta, fresh pasta, filled pasta, and baked pasta dishes, as well as giving you some basic recipes for making your own fresh pasta and sauces. I hope you will enjoy recreating some of my favorite recipes, from the traditional classics to more updated versions of Italy's greatest food.

HOW TO COOK PERFECT PASTA

Make sure you use a large saucepan filled with plenty of water; pasta needs room to move around when cooking.

Use 4¼ cups (1 liter) of water for every 3½ oz (100 g) of pasta.

Bring a large saucepan of water, covered with a lid, to a boil. When the water is just beginning to boil, remove the lid and add salt.

Use 1½–2 teaspoons of salt for every 4¼ cups (1 liter) of water. This might seem like a lot, but the pasta really needs this flavor boost!

When the water is vigorously boiling, add the pasta and stir with a wooden spoon to avoid it sticking. Do not cover with a lid.

Cook the pasta until slightly underdone or, as Italians like to say, *al dente*. This literally means "to the tooth"—it should be soft enough to eat but still retain a little bite. This way, the pasta takes longer to chew, which gives you more time to taste and enjoy and, thereafter, digest it properly. There really is nothing worse than overcooked pasta!

When cooking dried pasta, check the directions on the package for timings—I almost always reduce that time by a couple of minutes. Keep tasting until it is cooked to your liking. Fresh pasta, such as *spaghetti* or *tagliatelle*, takes just a minute or two, and fresh filled pasta just a bit longer. Again, taste until satisfied.

Always keep a little of the pasta cooking water aside before draining—just ladle a few spoonfuls out into a bowl. You may not always need it, but adding a little of the cooking water will loosen sauces so that they coat the pasta better, making it nice and glossy.

Drain the pasta in a colander. Alternatively, you can use tongs for long pasta and a "spider," pasta fork, or slotted spoon for short pasta, to transfer the cooked pasta immediately to the sauce.

MATCHING PASTA SHAPES TO SAUCES

Italians are so very particular about what pasta shape should be served with what sauce. And, although it might sound absurd, it is actually true—certain shapes just go better with certain sauces. As an Italian, you grow up with this and instinctively know, just by looking at a shape, what sort of sauce would go with it.

Basically, try to match long, thin pasta shapes, such as *spaghetti* or *linguine*, to quick, light sauces, such as a simple tomato sauce, or serve with fish. Short, thick shapes like *penne* or *rigatoni*, marry well with heavier, more robust-tasting sauces and ragùs; the ridges on these shapes help the thicker sauces cling to the pasta. Contrary to popular belief, *spaghetti* doesn't go with Bolognese sauce—it is just too thin and the thick ragù simply falls off the strands. Italians eat this with *tagaliatelle* or *pappardelle*, since the meat sauce can cling to the thicker strands. In southern Italy, our traditional meat ragù is eaten with thick, ridged *rigatoni* or long, thick *ziti*.

Small shapes such as *farfalle* or *fusilli* are perfect for salads. Italians use smaller *ditalini* or *macaroni* for thick vegetable and bean soups. The really small shapes, collectively known as *pastina*, including *stelline* (small stars) or alphabet shapes, are the perfect addition to light broths. As well as classic *cannelloni*, shapes such as *conchiglioni* (large shells) and *paccheri* (large tubes), are all used for filling and creating wonderful baked dishes.

Of course, shapes and sauces are also very dependent on region, climate, and what produce is grown locally. For instance, *pesto Genovese* originated in Liguria, where sweet-smelling basil grows in abundance and the region's delicate olive oil is perfect for making this sauce. In cooler northern Italy, creamy butter and cheese sauces are more common, as opposed to the south where tomatoes rule. Is this way, pasta shapes and pasta dishes evolved to suit the available ingredients, giving us the huge variety of pasta shapes that we are lucky to have on the market these days.

QUICK GUIDE TO POPULAR SHAPE/SAUCE COMBINATIONS

CONCHIGLIE
tomato-based sauces

CONCHIGLIONI – large shells
filled and baked

FARFALLE
light vegetable and fish sauces; pesto; salads

FUSILLI
pesto; light tomato and olive sauces; baked dishes

LINGUINE
pesto; light fish and shellfish

MACARONI
bean soups; minestrone; cheesy bakes

ORECCHIETTE
tomato sauces; broccoli with extra-virgin olive oil and chili (typical of Puglia); meat ragù

PACCHERI
meat ragù; baked dishes

PAPPARDELLE
Bolognese ragù; game; mushrooms

PASTINA – small stars, *orzo*, *farfalline* (little butterflies), *anellini* (little rings), alphabet shapes
light broths and soups

PENNE
veggie tomato sauces; arrabbiata sauces; vegetables

RIGATONI
meaty ragùs; baked dishes

SPAGHETTI
light tomato sauces; shellfish (e.g. clams); carbonara sauces; broken up in soups

SPIRALI
pesto; light tomato sauces; baked dishes

TAGLIATELLE
Bolognese ragù; mushrooms; game

DRIED PASTA

This is the chapter to which I've dedicated the most recipes. Dried pasta is just so versatile, quick and easy to cook, and can be made in a different way every day. Like all Italians, I always keep a good selection in my pantry—at least a couple of varieties of *pasta lunga* (long pasta) such as *spaghetti*, *linguine*, and *tagliatelle*; *pasta corta* (short pasta) such as *penne*, *farfalle*, and *rigatoni*; as well as tiny shapes for soups. Along with some pantry essentials and fresh produce, I know I can rustle up a satisfying meal in no time.

There is such a huge variety of dried pasta shapes on the market these days. In Italy, you really are spoiled for choice, with over 650 different types to choose from! Even the ubiquitous *spaghetti* comes in many varieties, from thin *spaghettini* to thicker *spaghettoni*. I love to discover new shapes and imagine how I will cook them.

Cooking times for dried pasta vary greatly, depending on size, shape, and brand. This is why I haven't put cooking times in any of the recipes in this chapter and suggest you check the cooking directions on your package. I like my pasta to be very *al dente,* so I always reduce the cooking times stated and do several taste tests along the way.

I find the quality Italian pasta brands, which take a little longer to cook, are really worth paying a little bit extra for. The producers use good-quality durum wheat flour and adhere to strict rules and regulations on the making and drying of the pasta. Look out for pasta that has been "bronze-cut," meaning the shapes have been cut with traditional bronze molds; this makes the pasta shapes coarser, giving them the classic rough texture that sauces can better cling to, which in turn ensures you enjoy every mouthful. Don't be tempted to buy the cheaper "quick cook" varieties, and always go for the best quality you can—it really will make a huge difference to your final dish.

INSALATA PRIMAVERILE DI FUSILLI, FAVE, PISELLI E PECORINO

Spring Pasta Salad with Fresh Fava Beans, Peas, and Pecorino

Even though peas and fava beans are widely available frozen, there is nothing I love more during the spring than enjoying these vegetables in their freshest form. In rural Italy, fava beans are eaten raw with pecorino cheese, which gave me the inspiration for this pasta salad.

Serves 4

11½ oz (325 g) *fusilli bucati corti* pasta

1¼ cups (5½ oz/150 g) fresh fava beans (shelled weight; peeled if you like)

1 cup (5½ oz/150 g) fresh peas (shelled weight)

⅓ cup (80 ml) extra-virgin olive oil, plus extra for drizzling

⅔ cup (2 oz/60 g) grated pecorino, plus extra shavings to serve

2 slices of prosciutto, finely chopped

1 garlic clove, very finely chopped or minced

½ handful of mint or basil leaves, very finely chopped

sea salt and freshly ground black pepper

Bring a large saucepan of salted water to a boil and cook the *fusilli bucati corti* until *al dente* (check the instructions on your package for cooking time).

Meanwhile, blanch the fava beans in boiling water for about 5 minutes until tender but not mushy, then drain and set aside to cool. Peel off the skins, if desired. Likewise, blanch the peas for about 3 minutes until tender but not mushy, then drain and set aside to cool.

In a small bowl, combine the olive oil, grated pecorino, prosciutto, garlic, and mint. Season with a little black pepper and set aside.

Drain the pasta, stir in a drizzle of olive oil (to prevent sticking) and leave to cool.

In a large bowl, combine the cooled pasta with the fava beans, peas, and the dressing mixture, and serve with extra shavings of pecorino.

Dried Pasta

INSALATA DI PASTA ALLA PUTTANESCA

Puttanesca Pasta Salad

This pasta salad has all the ingredients of a typical *puttanesca* sauce, but used raw. It uses typical Italian pantry staples, so is easy to make at any time, although it is particularly delicious during the summer months. Any leftovers can be packed in your lunchbox the next day.

Serves 4

11½ oz (325 g) *casarecce* pasta

3¼ cups (1 lb 2 oz/500 g) baby plum tomatoes, halved

10 black olives

10 green olives

1 tablespoon capers

5 anchovy fillets

1 garlic clove, finely chopped

1 teaspoon dried oregano

½ red chili pepper (optional)

¼ cup (60 ml) extra-virgin olive oil, plus extra for drizzling

a handful of basil leaves

sea salt

Bring a large saucepan of salted water to a boil and cook the *casarecce* until *al dente* (check the instructions on your package for cooking time).

Meanwhile, combine the tomatoes, olives, capers, anchovies, garlic, oregano, chili (if using), olive oil, and some salt, to taste. Set aside.

Drain the pasta, drizzle with a little olive oil, and leave to cool.

Mix the cooled pasta with the tomato salad, add the basil leaves, and let rest for 5 minutes before serving. Store in the refrigerator if not using immediately.

INSALATA DI FARFALLE CON ZUCCHINE E GAMBERETTI

Pasta Salad with Baby Zucchini and Shrimp

A deliciously light pasta salad that is perfect during the spring and summer months when baby zucchini are at their best. It can be made in advance and enjoyed at picnics or parties.

Serves 4

11½ oz (325 g) *farfalle* pasta

4 baby zucchini, very thinly sliced (julienned)

7 oz (200 g) cooked peeled jumbo shrimp

5 baby plum tomatoes, halved

¼ cup (60 ml) extra-virgin olive oil, plus extra for drizzling

a handful of basil leaves

sea salt

Bring a large saucepan of salted water to a boil and cook the *farfalle* until *al dente* (check the instructions on your package for cooking time).

In a large bowl, combine the zucchini strips with the shrimp, tomatoes, olive oil, and basil. Season with some salt, cover with plastic wrap, and leave to marinate until the pasta is cooked.

Drain the pasta, drizzle with a little olive oil (to prevent sticking), mix well, and leave to cool.

Once the pasta has cooled, combine it with the other ingredients. Serve immediately or keep in the refrigerator until required. Bring back to room temperature before serving.

INSALATA DI PASTA INVERNALE

Winter Pasta Salad

A quick and simple pasta salad with winter radicchio. The sweet pears marry well with the slightly bitter radicchio and rich gooey Gorgonzola, and the walnuts add a nice crunchiness. Excellent for a nourishing lunch that can be made in advance and eaten on-the-go.

Serves 4

10 oz (280 g) *ruote (rotelle)* pasta

extra-virgin olive oil, for drizzling

2 cups (3 oz/85 g) sliced radicchio

1 Anjou or Bosc pear, peeled and thinly sliced

½ cup (2 oz/60 g) coarsely chopped walnuts

3½ oz (100 g) Gorgonzola cheese, crumbled

balsamic vinegar, for drizzling

sea salt and freshly ground black pepper

Bring a large saucepan of salted water to a boil and cook the pasta until *al dente* (check the instructions on your package for cooking time). Drain, rinse under cold water, then drain again. Mix in a drizzle of extra-virgin olive oil to stop the pasta from sticking, and set aside to cool.

Meanwhile, prepare the other salad ingredients.

Combine the cooled pasta with the radicchio, pear slices, walnuts, and Gorgonzola, drizzle with a little extra-virgin olive oil and balsamic vinegar, and sprinkle with a little salt and pepper to taste.

PASTACINI

Pasta Croquettes

This is pasta's equivalent to risotto's *arancini*. They are delicious to make for a snack at any time and can also be made with leftover cooked pasta. They can be a bit messy to make, but kids will love to help out!

Makes 8 croquettes

4½ oz (125 g) *tagliatelle* pasta

2 tablespoons (1 oz/30 g) butter

⅓ cup (1 oz/30 g) grated Parmesan

all-purpose flour, for dusting
and coating

1 oz (30 g) cooked ham, finely chopped

1¾ oz (50 g) fresh mozzarella, drained and
chopped into small cubes

2 eggs

sea salt

breadcrumbs, for coating

vegetable oil, for deep-frying

grated Parmesan or pecorino, for sprinkling
(optional)

Bring a large saucepan of salted water to a boil and cook the *tagliatelle* until *al dente* (check the instructions on your package for cooking time). Drain well and combine with the butter and grated Parmesan. Set aside to cool.

Lightly dust a work surface with flour. When cool, roughly chop the *tagliatelle* and divide into 8 portions. Place some cooked ham and mozzarella cubes onto each portion then, using your hands, mold each portion into a croquette-type shape. Tightly wrap each croquette in plastic wrap and place in the freezer for 20 minutes to firm up.

Put some flour onto a plate for coating. Beat the eggs in a bowl and set it nearby. Then heap abundant breadcrumbs on another plate and set it nearby. Unwrap each croquette and roll in the flour until well coated, then dip in the beaten egg, and finally coat with breadcrumbs.

In a deep, heavy pan, heat enough vegetable oil for deep-frying until very hot (it is ready when a cube of bread browns in 30 seconds). Fry the croquettes in the hot oil for 3–4 minutes until golden-brown on all sides. Remove with a slotted spoon, drain on paper towels, and enjoy hot, sprinkled with cheese, if you like.

Dried Pasta

FRITTATA DI PASTA AVANZATA

Leftover Pasta Frittata

This is a tasty way to make use of leftover pasta and any other ingredients you might want to use up, such as cheese, cured meats, or grilled veggies. In the Italian kitchen, this has long been made to deal with pasta leftovers, but nowadays it is specially made in mini portions and sold as street food.

Serves 4

3 eggs

1¼ cups (4½ oz/125 g) grated Parmesan

6 tablespoons (3 oz/85 g) butter, melted

10 basil leaves, roughly torn

10 baby plum tomatoes, or ¼ cup (60 ml) leftover tomato sauce

leftovers, such as pieces of ham, salami, other cheeses, and/or grilled vegetables (optional)

12 oz (350 g) cooked pasta (leftovers are fine)

3 tablespoons extra-virgin olive oil

sea salt and freshly ground black pepper

a handful of arugula, to garnish (optional)

In a large bowl, beat the eggs, then stir in the grated Parmesan, melted butter, basil leaves, tomatoes or tomato sauce, and any other leftovers you like. Season with a little salt and black pepper, then combine well with the cooked pasta.

Heat the olive oil in a large ovenproof non-stick frying pan over medium heat, pour in the mixture, and cook as you would an omelet for 4–5 minutes, until the bottom is set firm. Carefully flip the frittata onto a large plate if you can, then slide it back into the pan to cook the other side for another 4–5 minutes. Alternatively, place under a hot broiler until golden.

Serve hot or cold, garnished with arugula, if desired.

MINESTRONE GENOVESE

Minestrone with Pesto

This soup was originally made with fresh homegrown produce and offered to sailors docking at Genova so that they could enjoy fresh food after being away at sea. Traditionally, the vegetables were boiled and the soup was made so thick you could stand a spoon in it! If there was any left over, it was sliced and fried. My version is not so thick and I like to sweat the vegetables to obtain more flavor. That said, if your veggies are of the freshest homegrown quality, then simply boiling them will be fine. The addition of pesto gives this soup a lovely green color, as well as the aromatic flavor of basil.

Serves 4–6

¼ cup (60 ml) extra-virgin olive oil

1 large onion, finely chopped

1 celery stalk, finely chopped

1 large carrot, finely chopped

1 small zucchini, cut into
 small chunks

1 large potato, peeled and cut into
 small chunks

5 oz (140 g) Swiss chard, finely chopped
 (including stalks)

2 fresh plum tomatoes, seeded and diced

6⅓ cups (1.5 liters) hot vegetable stock

1 x 14 oz (400 g) can of borlotti beans, drained

4 oz (120 g) thick *spaghetti* pasta, broken into
 2 in (5 cm) pieces

1 quantity of Basil Pesto (see page 168)

freshly ground black pepper

Heat the olive oil in a large saucepan over medium heat. Add the onion, celery, and carrot, and sweat for 2–3 minutes until softened. Stir in the zucchini, potato, Swiss chard, and tomatoes, and continue to sauté for 1 minute or so. Add the stock, season with some black pepper, and then cover with a lid, increase the heat, and bring to a boil. Reduce the heat and simmer, covered, for about 15 minutes until the vegetables are cooked but not mushy.

Stir in the borlotti beans and cook for 2 minutes. Increase the heat and bring to a boil, then add the *spaghetti* pieces. Reduce the heat and simmer until the pasta is cooked *al dente* (check the instructions on your package for cooking time).

Remove from the heat, let rest for about 3 minutes, then stir in the pesto and serve.

ZUPPA DI VERDURE E PASTINA

Vegetable and Pastina Soup

This should be really be called "Olivia's Soup," since it's my daughter Olivia's favorite meal! Small pasta shapes (*pastina*) can be little stars, butterflies, alphabet shapes, or even broken-up *capelli d'angelo* (angel hair pasta) if you have nothing else. In Italy, there is a huge variety of *pastina* shapes to choose from and we always bring some back after a trip. For an even richer flavor, *pastina* can be made with homemade broths (such as the Three-Meat Broth on page 112) in place of the ready-made vegetable stock.

Serves 4

3 tablespoons extra-virgin olive oil

½ onion, finely chopped

⅓ celery stalk, finely chopped

1 carrot, finely chopped

⅔ cup (3 oz/85 g) finely chopped zucchini

3½ cups (800 ml) hot vegetable stock

generous 1 cup (3 oz/85 g) *pastina* (small pasta shapes)

grated Parmesan, to serve (optional)

Heat the olive oil in a saucepan over medium heat. Add the onion, celery, carrot, and zucchini, and sweat for 2–3 minutes until softened. Pour in the vegetable stock, bring to a boil, then reduce the heat and gently simmer for 5 minutes. Add the *pastina* and cook until *al dente* (check the instructions on your package for cooking time).

Divide among serving bowls and serve immediately with a sprinkling of grated Parmesan, if desired.

ZUPPA DI LENTICCHIE CON DITALINI E RICOTTA SALATA

Lentil Soup with Ditalini and Ricotta Salata

Quick and simple one-pot cooking—ideal for those busy midweek evenings. A lentil and pasta soup is always a favorite in my household, especially during cooler months. The sprinkling of chopped herbs and salty *ricotta salata* to finish adds some freshness to this comfort food dish. *Ricotta salata* is now widely available in good Italian delis, but if you prefer you can substitute grated Parmesan.

Serves 4

1½ cups (10½ oz/300 g) French green or brown lentils, picked over and rinsed

1 celery stalk with leaves, finely chopped

1 carrot, finely chopped

1 potato, cut into small chunks

6 baby plum tomatoes, halved

1 garlic clove, left whole

2 tablespoons extra-virgin olive oil, plus extra for drizzling

8½ cups (2 liters) vegetable stock

1 cup (2¾ oz/75 g) *ditalini* pasta

sea salt and freshly ground black pepper

1 tablespoon chopped thyme and marjoram leaves, to serve

3 oz (85 g) *ricotta salata*, grated, to serve

Put the lentils, celery, carrot, potato, tomatoes, garlic clove, olive oil, and vegetable stock into a large saucepan. Cover with a lid and bring to a boil. Reduce the heat and simmer gently for about 20–30 minutes, until the lentils are tender (check the instructions on your lentil package for cooking time).

Add the *ditalini* and cook until the pasta is *al dente* (check the instructions on your pasta package for cooking time). Remove from the heat and check for seasoning, adding salt as necessary.

Divide among serving bowls, sprinkle with black pepper, the freshly chopped herbs, and the *ricotta salata,* and serve immediately.

CARBONARA MARE E MONTI

Carbonara from the Sea and Mountains

Mare e monti is a traditional pasta dish that includes both seafood, and produce from the land. The *carbonara* element of egg yolks and cream (although, strictly speaking, cream is not normally used) works really well with the clams, salami, and sun-dried tomatoes. Try it out for a delicious alternative to the more familiar kind served with bacon.

Serves 4

2¼ lb (1 kg) fresh clams

scant 1 cup (200 ml) white wine

12¾ oz (360 g) *spaghetti* pasta

salt

2 tablespoons extra-virgin olive oil

1 banana shallot, finely chopped

2 oz (60 g) spicy salami, chopped

1 cup (2 oz/60 g) sun-dried tomatoes, chopped

4 egg yolks

3½ tablespoons heavy cream

2 tablespoons finely chopped parsley

In a saucepan, combine the clams with the white wine, cover with a lid, and cook over medium heat for 2–3 minutes until the shells open. Turn off the heat and leave to cool slightly. When cool enough to handle, remove the flesh from the shells, discarding the shells as you go, and set aside, reserving the cooking liquid. You can leave a few clams intact for decoration if you like. Any unopened shells should be discarded.

Bring a large saucepan of salted water to a boil, and cook the *spaghetti* until *al dente* (check the instructions on your package for cooking time).

In the meantime, heat the oil in a large sauté pan over medium heat. Add the shallot and cook for a couple of minutes to soften. Add the salami and sun-dried tomatoes and cook for a further minute. Stir in the cooled clams with their cooking liquid and continue to cook over medium heat until the spaghetti is ready.

In a bowl, combine the egg yolks and cream and set aside.

Drain the pasta, add it to the clam sauce, and remove the pan from the heat. Quickly stir in the egg mixture, coating the pasta well, and serve immediately, garnished with the chopped parsley.

CAVATELLI CON FRUTTI DI MARE E CECI

Cavatelli with Shellfish and Chickpeas

Cavatelli are small pasta shells made with eggless pasta dough, available dried in good Italian delis. They combine perfectly with shellfish and legumes, as in this quick, simple, and delicious recipe. If you can't find *cavatelli*, you can substitute *gnocchetti sardi*.

Serves 4

1 lb 2 oz (500 g) fresh mussels

1 lb 2 oz (500 g) fresh clams

scant ½ cup (100 ml) white wine

10½ oz (300 g) *cavatelli* pasta

¼ cup (60 ml) extra-virgin olive oil, plus extra for drizzling

2 garlic cloves, finely chopped

1¾ cups (9 oz/250 g) cherry tomatoes, quartered

1 x 14 oz (400 g) can chickpeas, drained

a handful of parsley, finely chopped

sea salt

Wash the shellfish in plenty of cold water to remove any dirt, de-beard the mussels, and rinse well. Discard any shellfish with broken or open shells. Transfer to a large saucepan with the wine, cover with a tightly fitting lid, and cook over medium heat for 2–3 minutes, until all the shells have opened up (discard any that have not opened). Drain, reserving the cooking liquid.

If you wish, remove the flesh from about three-quarters of the shellfish and set aside, keeping the remaining shellfish in their shells for decoration. Alternatively, remove all the shellfish from their shells.

Bring a large saucepan of salted water to a boil and cook the pasta until *al dente* (check the instructions on your package for cooking time).

Heat the olive oil in a large frying pan set over medium heat. Add the garlic and sweat for 1 minute, then add the tomatoes and fry, stirring, for a further minute. Add all the shellfish (taking care that any shells do not break), the chickpeas, three-quarters of the parsley, and a scant 1 cup (200 ml) of the shellfish cooking liquid, and continue to cook for about 5 minutes. Check for seasoning and, if necessary, add a little salt.

Drain the pasta, reserving a little of the cooking water. Add the pasta to the shellfish sauce with a little more of the shellfish liquid or pasta cooking water, increase the heat, and cook for 1 minute. Remove from the heat and serve sprinkled with the remaining parsley and a drizzle of extra-virgin olive oil.

LINGUINE AL CARTOCCIO CON GAMBERI E PESTO

Steam-Baked Linguine with Jumbo Shrimp and Pesto

This light pasta, steam-baked with jumbo shrimp, will surely delight your guests as they open their parcels of delicious goodness! Steam-baking is not only a feast for the eyes, but a lovely, light way of cooking that locks all the flavors in. I have used pre-foiled parchment paper, but if you can't find it, use a sheet of parchment paper inside a sheet of foil and make sure you wrap tightly so that none of the juices can escape during cooking.

Serves 4

12 oz (350 g) *linguine* pasta

⅔ cup (150 ml) Basil Pesto (see page 168 or use a ready-made variety)

extra-virgin olive oil, for drizzling

8 raw, shell-on jumbo shrimp, cleaned

½ cup (125 ml) white wine

sea salt and freshly ground black pepper

4 slices of lemon and a few basil leaves, to garnish

Preheat the oven to 400°F (200°C).

Bring a large saucepan of salted water to a boil and cook the pasta for half of the cooking time stated on the package. Drain well, mix with half of the pesto sauce, and set aside.

Spread 4 foil-lined parchment paper sheets out on your work surface (foil-side down), and drizzle each with a little extra-virgin olive oil. Divide the *linguine* into 4 portions and place a portion onto each sheet, top each with 2 shrimp, followed by the remaining pesto and a little salt and pepper. Drizzle white wine and a little extra-virgin olive oil over each portion. Wrap the parcels well, place on a baking sheet, and bake in the hot oven for 12 minutes.

Remove from the oven and serve the parcels on a platter or on individual plates, with a slice of lemon each and a few basil leaves to garnish.

LINGUINE ALLE VONGOLE

Linguine with Clams

Pasta with clams is a favorite dish in coastal resorts all over Italy. For a real taste of the sea, get fresh clams from your fishmonger—it will make all the difference. Once the clams have been thoroughly cleaned, the recipe is very simple and extremely quick to prepare.

Serves 4

2 lb 4 oz (1 kg) fresh clams

3 tablespoons extra-virgin olive oil, plus extra for drizzling

2 garlic cloves, finely sliced

8 cherry tomatoes, halved

a handful of chopped parsley

⅔ cup (150 ml) white wine

sea salt

Wash the clams thoroughly under cold running water to remove impurities, then place in a bowl, cover with plenty of cold salted water, and soak for 2 hours—this helps to further purge the clams of impurities.

Rinse the soaked clams under cold running water and set aside.

Bring a large saucepan of salted water to a boil and cook the *linguine* until *al dente* (check the instructions on your package for cooking time).

Heat the olive oil in a large saucepan over medium heat, add the garlic, tomatoes, and half of the parsley, and cook for 1 minute. Add the clams and sauté for 1 minute, then pour in the white wine, cover, and cook for 2 minutes, or until the clam shells have opened up. Discard any clams that remained closed.

Drain the pasta, add it to the clams, and sauté for 1 minute, mixing until well amalgamated. Remove from the heat and serve immediately, sprinkled with the remaining chopped parsley and a drizzle of extra-virgin olive oil.

SPAGHETTINI AROMATICI

Anchovy-Infused Spaghettini with Capers and Olives

This is lovely light and summery dish, where only a few of the ingredients need cooking. I have opted for the thinner variety of *spaghetti*, since the sauce clings to it better. The combination of cooked anchovies with the raw herbs, capers, and olives gives a lovely fresh flavor and kick to the dish.

Serves 4

12 oz (350 g) *spaghettini* pasta

¼ cup (60 ml) extra-virgin olive oil, plus extra for drizzling

1 garlic clove, squashed

4 anchovy fillets, finely chopped

1½ teaspoon capers, finely chopped

10 black olives, pitted and finely chopped

a handful of flat-leaf parsley, chopped

6 mint leaves, finely chopped

sea salt

Bring a large saucepan of salted water to a boil and cook the *spaghettini* until *al dente* (check the instructions on your package for cooking time).

Meanwhile, heat the olive oil in a frying pan over medium heat, add the garlic, and cook for about 1 minute, or until it begins to color. Remove and discard the garlic, then add the anchovies and cook until the anchovies dissolve. Remove from the heat and stir in the capers, olives, and chopped herbs.

Drain the *spaghettini* and toss with the sauce. Serve immediately, with a drizzle of extra-virgin olive oil to finish.

BUCATINI CON LE SARDE E FINOCCHIETTO

Bucatini with Fresh Sardines and Wild Fennel

The secret of this classic Sicilian dish is in the flavor of the fennel. Pungent wild fennel is best for this—you can obtain it from good grocery stores, farmers' markets, or forage for it yourself (it grows wild throughout the Mediterranean, UK, and US). If you can't get wild fennel, use the hairy green fronds of fennel bulbs (don't waste the fennel bulb either; finely sliced and dressed with extra-virgin olive oil, salt, and black pepper, it can be served as a refreshing side dish to the pasta). The crunchy breadcrumb topping is a typical "poor man's" substitute for grated Parmesan, and works perfectly with this pasta dish.

Serves 4

1 large handful of wild fennel or
    the fronds of 2 fennel bulbs, plus extra to
    garnish

¼ cup (60 ml) extra-virgin olive oil

1 large onion, finely chopped

1 teaspoon saffron, ground to powder

¼ cup (1½ oz/40 g) pine nuts

¼ cup (1½ oz/40 g) golden raisins, soaked in a
    little warm water

5 anchovy fillets

5½ oz (150 g) fresh sardines, cleaned, heads
    and innards removed, chopped into chunks

10½ oz (300 g) *bucatini* pasta

sea salt

For the topping:

1 tablespoon extra-virgin olive oil

1 garlic clove, left whole

¾ cup (1½ oz/40 g) breadcrumbs

Put the wild fennel or fennel fronds in a large saucepan of water and bring to a boil, then remove from the heat and set aside to let the fennel infuse the water. This water will be used to cook the pasta.

Heat the olive oil in a large saucepan over medium heat, add the onion, and sweat for about 5 minutes until softened. Stir in the saffron, pine nuts, drained raisins, and anchovy fillets, and cook over low–medium heat until the anchovy fillets have melted. Add the sardine chunks, increase the heat, and cook, stirring, for 2 minutes, adding a splash of the fennel-infused water.

Remove the fennel from the water, cool slightly, and finely chop. Set aside.

Add a little salt to the fennel-infused water, bring to a boil, and cook the *bucatini* pasta until *al dente* (check the instructions on your package for cooking time).

Meanwhile, make the topping: heat the olive oil in a small pan over medium heat, add the garlic clove, and sweat for 1 minute, then add the breadcrumbs. Cook, stirring all the time, until the oil has been absorbed and the breadcrumbs are golden. Remove from the heat, discard the garlic clove, and set aside.

Drain the pasta, reserving a little of the cooking water. Add the pasta and reserved cooking water to the sauce in the pan, then add the chopped fennel and mix together over high heat until well combined. Serve immediately with the breadcrumb topping sprinkled over and a garnish of fennel fronds, if desired.

Dried Pasta

MEZZI PACCHERI CON COZZE E LIMONE

Mezzi Paccheri with Mussels and Lemon

I love this dish, which combines the taste of the sea, my beloved Amalfi lemons, and one of my favorite pasta shapes. *Mezzi paccheri* are a large tubular-shaped Neapolitan pasta, about half the length of *paccheri*. The addition of the baked mussels gives this dish a nice crunchiness.

Serves 4

2 lb 4 oz (1 kg) fresh mussels

scant ½ cup (100 ml) white wine

11½ oz (325 g) *mezzi paccheri* pasta

1 tablespoon finely chopped parsley

2 tablespoons breadcrumbs

8 cherry tomatoes, halved

2 tablespoons extra-virgin olive oil, plus extra for drizzling

1 garlic clove, left whole

8 oz (240 g) zucchini, sliced into very thin strips

1 small lemon: zest cut into thin strips to garnish, then juiced

sea salt

Preheat the oven to 350°F (180°C).

Wash the mussels in plenty of cold water to remove any dirt, de-beard if necessary, and rinse well. Discard any mussels with broken or open shells. Transfer to a large saucepan with the white wine, cover with a tightly fitting lid, and cook over medium heat for 2–3 minutes until the shells have opened up. Discard any shells that have not opened. Reserve the cooking liquid. Remove the flesh from about three-quarters of the mussels and set aside, keeping about 12 mussels in their shells.

Bring a large saucepan of salted water to a boil and cook the pasta until *al dente* (check the instructions on your package for cooking time).

Meanwhile, place the mussels in their shells on a baking sheet, top with chopped parsley, breadcrumbs, and the cherry tomato halves, drizzle with some extra-virgin olive oil, and bake in the hot oven for about 5 minutes, until golden.

Heat 2 tablespoons extra-virgin olive oil in a frying pan over medium heat, add the garlic, and sweat for 1 minute, then add the zucchini and sauté for 2–3 minutes until tender. Discard the garlic clove. Add the shelled mussels and a couple of tablespoons of the reserved mussel cooking liquid.

Drain the pasta and add it to the sauce with the lemon juice. Mix well, and sauté for a minute or so over medium–high heat, adding a little more of the mussel cooking liquid if necessary.

Remove from the heat, divide among serving plates, and top with the baked mussels and lemon zest. Serve immediately.

MEZZE MANICHE CON RAGU DI MOSCARDINI

Mezze Maniche with Baby Octopus Ragù

This popular dish, eaten along the coast in southern Italy and Sicily, has always been a family favorite. Use fresh or frozen baby octopus for a quick and delicious meal. *Mezze maniche* means "short sleeves," named for its short, cylindrical shape, and it is perfect with this robust sauce.

Serves 4

3 tablespoons extra-virgin olive oil

2 garlic cloves, finely chopped

1 red chili pepper, finely chopped

3 anchovy fillets

1 lb 9 oz (700 g) baby octopus, rinsed and dried

1 lb 2 oz (500 g) baby plum tomatoes, halved

a handful of fresh parsley, finely chopped

10½ oz (300 g) *mezze maniche* pasta

sea salt

Heat the olive oil in a large frying pan over medium heat, add the garlic, chili, and anchovy fillets, and cook for 1 minute or so until the anchovies dissolve. Add the baby octopus and sauté for 1 minute. Add the tomatoes and half of the parsley, then reduce the heat, cover with a lid, and cook for 20 minutes.

Meanwhile, bring a large saucepan of salted water to a boil and cook the *mezze maniche* until *al dente* (check the instructions on your package for cooking time).

Drain the pasta, add it to the sauce, and sauté for 1 minute over medium–high heat until well combined. Remove from the heat and serve sprinkled with the remaining parsley.

SPAGHETTI ALLA CARRETTIERA

Cart Driver's Spaghetti

This hearty Sicilian recipe was traditionally made for cart drivers transporting goods. Often the journeys were long and arduous, so pasta and long-lasting ingredients like dried funghi and preserved tuna were brought along to sustain them during their time away. This is still a popular dish for using up fresh produce like mushrooms alongside pantry staples. Quick and simple to prepare, it is a delicious, nourishing meal.

Serves 4

3 tablespoons extra-virgin olive oil

2 garlic cloves, finely chopped

½ red chili pepper, finely chopped

9 oz (250 g) mushrooms, thinly sliced

1 oz (30 g) dried porcini, reconstituted in a little warm water, then drained

2¾ cups (14 oz/400 g) baby plum tomatoes, halved

1 x 5 oz (140 g) can tuna, drained

11½ oz (325 g) *spaghetti* pasta

1½ cups (3½ oz/100 g) breadcrumbs

a handful of parsley, very finely chopped

sea salt

Heat 2 tablespoons of the olive oil in a frying pan over medium heat. Add the garlic and chili, and sweat for 1 minute, taking care not to burn. Add the mushrooms and the drained porcini, and sauté for about 3 minutes. Stir in the tomatoes, along with a little salt, and continue to cook for about 15 minutes. Stir in the tuna and heat through.

Meanwhile, bring a large saucepan of salted water to a boil and cook the *spaghetti* until *al dente* (check the instructions on your package for cooking time).

In a separate frying pan, heat the remaining olive oil, add the breadcrumbs and chopped parsley, and cook for 2 minutes over medium heat, until the breadcrumbs absorb the oil and become golden and crunchy—be careful not to burn them! Set aside.

Drain the *spaghetti*, add it to the sauce, and mix well over high heat for 1 minute. Remove from the heat and serve, sprinkled with the breadcrumb mixture.

Dried Pasta

LA GENOVESE DI TONNO CON ZITI

Ziti with Slow-Cooked Tuna and Onions

La Genovese is an ancient sauce that originated in Naples, where onions are slow-cooked until they become lovely and sweet. Traditionally, a piece of meat like veal, pork, or beef is used, but this relatively new idea of using tuna is popular in the village of Cetara on the Amalfi Coast, as well as in Sicily where fresh tuna is eaten in abundance. You could cook a whole piece of tuna, but I find using a couple of thick steaks is just fine and, surprisingly, the tuna does remain intact during cooking. At the end of cooking, gently break up the tuna and divide into 4 servings. Broken-up *ziti* (long, thick pasta tubes) are used here, but you could substitute *pennette*.

Serves 4

⅓ cup (80 ml) extra-virgin olive oil

2 anchovy fillets

1 celery stalk, finely chopped

1 carrot, finely chopped

2 lb 4 oz (1 kg) onions, finely sliced

9 oz (250 g) fresh tuna (whole piece or steaks)

¼ cup (60 ml) white wine

11½ oz (325 g) *ziti* pasta, broken up

sea salt and freshly gound black pepper

Heat the olive oil in a large saucepan, add the anchovy fillets, and cook over medium heat until they have melted. Add the celery and carrot, and sweat for 1 minute. Add the onions and some salt and pepper, lower the heat, cover with a lid, and cook gently for 20 minutes. Add the tuna and white wine, and continue to cook, covered, on a low heat for 2 hours, checking from time to time. (If necessary, add a little hot water or vegetable stock, although I find the onions usually release enough liquid to keep everything moist.)

Near the end of the cooking time, bring a large saucepan of salted water to a boil and cook the pasta until *al dente* (check the instructions on your package for cooking time).

Carefully remove the tuna and set aside. Drain the pasta, add to the onion sauce, and mix well to combine. Remove from the heat and serve with the tuna.

BIRBONI ATTERRATI

Wholewheat Tagliatelle with Anchovies and Walnuts

Birboni is an ancient pasta from the Amalfi Coast, the origins of which lie in the housewife's kitchen. Whenever fresh pasta was made, in order not to waste a thing, all the flour that did not end up in the pasta dough would be collected (even swept up from the floor!) and reused to make into more pasta. This became so popular that factories started to make a variety of tagliatelle, sold as "*birboni*." Obviously, it is now made with clean flour!

Birboni are usually combined with a few simple, local ingredients: anchovies and *Colatura di Alici*, a concentrated anchovy sauce that comes from the coastal village of Cetara. The sauce is available in Italian delis, however *birboni* are only obtainable in the local area, so I have substituted wholewheat *tagliatelle* here.

Serves 4

10½ oz (300 g) wholewheat *tagliatelle*
6 tablespoons extra-virgin olive oil
½ red chili pepper, finely chopped
4 garlic cloves, left whole
10 anchovy fillets
½ cup (2 oz/60 g) chopped walnuts
a handful of parsley, finely chopped
1 tablespoon *Colatura di Alici* (anchovy sauce)
sea salt

Bring a large saucepan of salted water to a boil and cook the pasta until *al dente* (check the instructions on your package for cooking time).

Meanwhile, heat the olive oil in a large sauté pan or frying pan set over medium heat. Add the chili and garlic, and sweat for 1 minute, then add the anchovy fillets and continue to cook until the anchovies have melted. Stir in the chopped walnuts, half of the parsley, and a couple of tablespoons of the pasta cooking water. Continue to cook, stirring occasionally, until the pasta is cooked. Remove and discard the garlic cloves.

Drain the *tagliatelle*, add it to the sauce, along with the *Colatura di Alici*, and mix well to combine. Remove from the heat and serve with the remaining parsley sprinkled over.

FARFALLE CON CARCIOFI E PANCETTA CROCCANTE

Farfalle with Artichokes and Crispy Pancetta

This quick and simple recipe uses tender artichoke hearts, which take no time to cook. In Italy, where artichokes are very popular, the hearts can be found in markets, ready-peeled and placed in buckets of acidulated water to avoid them turning black. The trend hasn't caught on elsewhere, but it really isn't difficult to prepare artichokes—once you've mastered the first one, it's child's play! For this recipe, choose the small purple variety, which are in season throughout spring from around February onwards.

Serves 4

11½ oz (325 g) *farfalle* pasta

8 small artichokes

juice of 2 small lemons

6 tablespoons extra-virgin olive oil, plus extra for drizzling

8 slices pancetta, finely sliced

2 banana shallots, finely chopped

6 tablespoons white wine

handful of parsley, chopped

sea salt and freshly ground black pepper

grated pecorino, to serve

Bring a large saucepan of salted water to a boil and cook the pasta until *al dente* (check the instructions on your package for cooking time).

Meanwhile, clean the artichokes by removing all the leaves until you get to the heart, slice in half and, with the help of a teaspoon, remove the hairy choke. Finely slice the hearts and place in a bowl of water acidulated with the lemon juice until you are ready to use.

Heat the olive oil in a frying pan, add the pancetta, and sauté over medium–high heat for 2–3 minutes until crispy. Add the shallots and sweat for 1 minute. Drain the artichokes, add to the pan, and fry, stirring, for about 2 minutes until softened but not mushy. Pour in the white wine and allow to evaporate, then season with salt and pepper.

Drain the pasta, reserving a little of the cooking water. Add the pasta to the sauce in the pan with a little of the reserved cooking water and mix well to combine. Stir in the chopped parsley. Remove from the heat, drizzle with a little extra-virgin olive oil, and serve with grated pecorino.

RIGATONI ALLA ZOZZANA

Rigatoni with Pancetta and Sausage

This robust Roman recipe takes its name from *zozza*, which in Roman dialect usually means "dirty," but in the case of this recipe means "rich," because all kinds of ingredients are added. It's a cross between the other classic Roman pasta dishes *cacio e pepe* and *carbonara*, and uses up all the typical leftovers, making it a substantial but extremely delicious dish.

Serves 4

10½ oz (300 g) *rigatoni* pasta

2 tablespoons extra-virgin olive oil

1 onion, finely chopped

3½ oz (100 g) pancetta, finely chopped

3½ oz (100 g) Italian pork sausage, skinned and crumbled

1 egg yolk

⅓ cup (1 oz/30 g) grated pecorino, plus extra for sprinkling

2 tablespoons light cream

sea salt and freshly ground black pepper

Bring a large saucepan of salted water to a boil and cook the pasta until *al dente* (check the instructions on your package for cooking time).

Heat the olive oil in a frying pan set over medium heat, add the onion, and sweat for 1 minute. Add the pancetta and sausage meat, and sauté for 10 minutes.

Meanwhile, in a small bowl, whisk together the egg yolk, grated pecorino, and cream, along with some salt and pepper.

Drain the cooked pasta, add it to the pan with the pancetta and sausage meat, mix well, and cook for 1 minute over high heat. Remove from the heat and mix in the creamy mixture. Serve immediately, with an extra sprinkling of black pepper and pecorino.

BUCATINI ALL'AMATRICIANA

Bucatini with Tomatoes and Guanciale

This classic Roman recipe originated in rural communities as a shepherd's dish and was originally made without tomatoes. When tomatoes were introduced to Italy, the recipe was finally recognized in the town of Amatrice, hence the name. *Amatriciana* sauce is often made with onions or garlic or pancetta, however this is the traditional version. *Guanciale* is a cured pork cheek obtainable from good Italian delis.

Serves 4

2 tablespoons extra-virgin olive oil

1 red chili pepper, left whole

6 oz (175 g) *guanciale* (cured pork cheek), rind removed, sliced into small, thick strips

¼ cup (60 ml) white wine

1 x 14 oz (400 g) can of chopped plum tomatoes

11½ oz (325 g) *bucatini* pasta

sea salt

abundant grated pecorino, to serve

Heat the olive oil in a large frying pan over medium heat, add the whole chili, and sweat for 1 minute, then stir in the *guanciale* and sauté for about 7 minutes, taking care not to burn. Add the white wine and allow to evaporate. At this point, remove the strips of *guanciale* and set aside. Add the tomatoes to the pan, along with a little salt, cover with a lid, and cook for a further 10 minutes.

Meanwhile, bring a large saucepan of salted water to a boil and cook the *bucatini* until *al dente* (check the instructions on your package for cooking time).

Return the *guanciale* to the tomato pan. Drain the pasta, add it to the pan, and cook over high heat for 1 minute or so. Remove from the heat, pick out and discard the chili, and serve with grated pecorino.

Dried Pasta

PACCHERI CON RAGU DI CARNE

Paccheri with Meat Ragù

Traditionally, the classic Neapolitan ragù would be made up of different types and cuts of meat, including pork ribs and sausages, and would be very slowly cooked for up to 6 hours or sometimes even overnight. I wanted to keep this simple, so have just used a piece of beef brisket, but the principle remains the same: the meat is slow-cooked in tomato sauce; the sauce is served with pasta as a first course, followed by the meat as a main course, with a green salad on the side. In southern Italy, Sunday would not be the same without a meat ragù for lunch.

Serves 4

3 tablespoons extra-virgin olive oil

1 onion, finely chopped

2 bay leaves

1 lb 10 oz (750 g) beef brisket, cut into large chunks

⅓ cup (80 ml) red wine

1 tablespoon tomato paste, dissolved in a little warm water

2 x 14 oz (400 g) cans of chopped plum tomatoes

a handful of basil leaves

3 tablespoons grated Parmesan, plus extra to serve

12 oz (350 g) *paccheri* pasta

sea salt and freshly ground black pepper

Heat the olive oil in a large saucepan over medium heat, add the onion and bay leaves, and sweat for about 3 minutes, until softened. Add the beef and sear well all over. Increase the heat, add the wine, and allow to evaporate. Stir in the tomato paste and chopped tomatoes, basil leaves, grated Parmesan, and some salt and pepper, and bring to a boil. Reduce the heat, cover with a lid, and simmer gently for 2 hours, stirring from time to time with a wooden spoon. Add a little hot water if the pan looks dry.

After 2 hours, check that the meat is cooked through and tender; if not, continue to cook until it is. Remove the meat and set aside, keeping it warm.

Bring a large saucepan of salted water to a boil, and cook the *paccheri* until *al dente* (check the instructions on your package for cooking time), then drain.

Place a little of the tomato sauce in a large serving bowl, followed by the *paccheri*, then top with the remaining tomato sauce and mix well. Serve immediately with the meat and a sprinkling of Parmesan. Alternatively, you can serve the meat as a main course with a green salad, if preferred.

GARGANELLI CON RAGU BIANCO DI VITELLO

Garganelli with Ground Veal

This is a quick and easy alternative for when you don't have time to make a slow-cooked Bolognese ragù. It is also delicious if you prefer a lighter sauce without tomatoes. I like the subtle taste of veal, which is widely used in Italian cooking, however you can substitute with organic ground pork if you like. *Garganelli* is an egg pasta rolled into small ridged tubes and it goes perfectly with this delicate sauce. Substitute with *penne* or *linguine,* if preferred.

Serves 4

12 oz (350 g) *garganelli* pasta

3 tablespoons extra-virgin olive oil

2 garlic cloves, very finely chopped

2 bay leaves

1 small carrot, very finely chopped

½ celery stalk, very finely chopped

12 oz (350 g) ground veal

scant ½ cup (100 ml) white wine

sea salt and freshly ground pepper

½ handful of parsley, finely chopped, to serve

grated pecorino, to serve

Bring a large saucepan of salted water to a boil and cook the *garganelli* until *al dente* (check the instructions on your package for cooking time).

Meanwhile, heat the olive oil in a large frying pan over medium heat, add the garlic, bay leaves, carrot, and celery, and sauté for 2 minutes. Stir in the veal and cook until well seared, adding a little salt and pepper to taste. Continue to sauté for about 10 minutes, then increase the heat, add the white wine, and allow to evaporate.

Drain the pasta, reserving a little of the cooking water. Add the pasta to the sauce and mix together over medium–high heat, adding a little of the pasta cooking water, until well combined. Remove from the heat and serve immediately, garnished with chopped parsley and grated pecorino.

FUSILLI CON CAVOLO NERO E SALSICCIA

Fusilli with Sausage and Cavolo Nero

This is a nutritious dish traditionally enjoyed during the winter months when *cavolo nero* is in abundance. For maximum flavor, use good-quality Italian pork sausages such as *luganica* (easily obtainable from Italian delis). Quick and simple to prepare, it's a great way of combining winter favorites for a comforting midweek supper.

Serves 4

14 oz (400 g) *cavolo nero* (lacinato kale), coarsely chopped

6 tablespoons extra-virgin olive oil, plus extra to serve

2 garlic cloves, left whole and squashed

1 red chili pepper, finely chopped (optional)

4 Italian pork sausages, skinnned and coarsely chopped

11½ oz (325 g) *fusilli bucati* pasta

sea salt

grated Parmesan, to serve

Bring a large saucepan of slightly salted water to a boil and cook the kale for about 10 minutes until softened. Drain, reserving the cooking water, and set aside.

Meanwhile, heat the olive oil in a frying pan over medium heat. Add the garlic and chili, and sweat for 1 minute, then add the sausage meat and fry, stirring, for about 5 minutes. Add the kale to the pan and continue to cook over medium–low heat while you cook the pasta.

Bring the kale cooking water back to a boil, adding more water if necessary, and cook the pasta in it until *al dente* (check the instructions on your package for cooking time).

Drain the cooked pasta, reserving a little of the cooking water. Add the pasta to the kale and sausage, along with a little of the cooking water, and mix well to combine.

Serve with a drizzle of extra-virgin olive oil and some grated Parmesan.

GIGLI CON PISELLI, PANCETTA E POMODORO FRESCO

Gigli with Peas, Pancetta, and Fresh Tomatoes

Gigli is a pretty lily-shaped pasta said to have originated in Florence, whose symbol is the lily flower. The combination of pancetta and peas is a perfect match—with the addition of colorful freshly chopped tomatoes and crunchy toasted pine nuts, this makes a perfect midweek family supper. If you can't find *gigli*, substitute *farfalle*.

Serves 4

4 vine tomatoes

12 oz (350 g) *gigli* pasta

1⅓ cups (7 oz/200 g) fresh peas (shelled weight)

½ cup (2 oz/60 g) pine nuts

2 tablespoons extra-virgin olive oil

3½ oz (100 g) pancetta, cubed

a handful of basil leaves

3 oz (85 g) Parmesan, shaved

sea salt and freshly ground black pepper

Bring a large saucepan of salted water to a boil.

Using a sharp knife, make a cross-shaped incision in the top of each tomato. Use a slotted spoon to lower them into the pan of boiling water for 20 seconds, then remove. When cool enough to handle, peel the tomatoes, cut into quarters, discard the seeds, and cut into small segments. Set aside.

Meanwhile, add the *gigli* pasta and fresh peas to the pan of boiling water and cook until the pasta is *al dente* (check the instructions on your package for cooking time).

Heat a dry frying pan over medium heat. When hot, add the pine nuts and toast for 2 minutes. Remove and set aside. In the same pan, heat the olive oil, add the pancetta, and sauté until crispy.

Drain the pasta and peas, and add them to the pan with the pancetta. Stir in the pine nuts, tomatoes, basil leaves, and half of the Parmesan. Season with some salt and pepper to taste and mix together well.

Remove from the heat and serve immediately, sprinkled with the remaining Parmesan.

ORECCHIETTE CON SALSICCIA E POMODORINI GIALLI

Orecchiette with Sausage and Baby Yellow Plum Tomatoes

Puglian dried *orecchiette* pasta is now widely available and ideal for this speedy dish. Make sure you get good quality Italian pork sausages and if you can't find yellow tomatoes, substitute with red ones.

Serves 4

14 oz (400 g) dried *orecchiette* pasta

3 tablespoons extra-virgin olive oil

1 garlic clove, left whole

½ red chili pepper, finely chopped

2 rosemary sprigs

9 oz (250 g) Italian pork sausages, skinned and crumbled

a splash of white wine

14 oz (400 g) baby yellow plum tomatoes, halved

sea salt

grated pecorino or Parmesan, to serve

Bring a large saucepan of salted water to a boil and cook the *orecchiette* until *al dente* (check the instructions on your package for cooking time).

Heat the olive oil in a large frying pan over medium heat, add the garlic, chili, and rosemary sprigs, and sweat for 1 minute or so, until the garlic begins to color. Remove and discard the garlic, then add the crumbled sausage and sauté for about 5 minutes until the sausage meat is golden all over. Add a splash of wine and allow to evaporate. Stir in the tomatoes, add a little salt to taste, and cook for 2 minutes.

Drain the pasta and add it to the frying pan, mixing well. Remove from the heat and serve immediately, sprinkled with grated pecorino or Parmesan.

PENNE CON PEPERONI ALLA TRAPANESE

Penne with Trapanese-Style Peppers

If you enjoy peppers, you will love this dish, which uses both yellow and red bell peppers cooked in two ways, as they do in the Trapani region of Sicily. It's nice to get the contrasting flavors of the roasted yellow peppers and sautéed red peppers.

Serves 4

3 yellow bell peppers
4 oval-shaped tomatoes, such as San Marzano
¼ cup (60 ml) extra-virgin olive oil
4 garlic cloves, finely chopped
1 red chili pepper, finely chopped
1 red bell pepper, thinly sliced
12 oz (350 g) *penne* pasta
a handful of parsley, finely chopped
1½ oz (40 g) pecorino, shaved
a handful of basil leaves, to serve
sea salt

Preheat the oven to 400°F (200°C).

Put the yellow bell peppers into a roasting pan and dry-roast in the hot oven for about 35 minutes, until the skin is golden-brown and the peppers have softened.

Meanwhile, bring some water to a boil. Submerge the tomatoes in the boiling water for 2 minutes, then drain. Remove the skins and seeds, and finely chop the flesh. Set aside.

When the yellow peppers are ready, carefully remove the skins and seeds, and roughly chop the flesh. Set aside.

Heat the olive oil in a large frying pan over medium heat, add the garlic and chili, and sweat for 1 minute. Add the red bell pepper and continue to cook for about 10 minutes, until the pepper has softened. Stir in the roasted yellow peppers and tomatoes, add some salt, and fry, stirring, over high heat for 1 minute. Reduce the heat to medium, cover with a lid, and cook for about 10 minutes, while you cook the pasta.

Bring a large saucepan of salted water to a boil and cook the pasta until *al dente* (check the instructions on your package for cooking time).

Drain the pasta, reserving a little of the cooking water. Add the pasta to the peppers, along with a little of the cooking water, and mix well to combine while still on the heat. Stir in the parsley, then remove from the heat and serve with shavings of pecorino cheese and basil leaves.

Dried Pasta

PENNE CON CAVOLFIORE ALLA PALERMITANA

Sicilian-Style Penne with Cauliflower

Sicilian cooking is all about simple, "*cucina povera*" food, given a kick with exotic North African-influenced ingredients. Cauliflower is much loved on the island, where it grows in abundance and is used in a lot of local dishes. In this recipe, the humble cauliflower is combined with raisins, pine nuts, saffron, capers, and olives for a delicious and nutritious dish.

Serves 4

1 lb 2 oz (500 g) cauliflower florets

6 tablespoons extra-virgin olive oil

4 anchovy fillets

1 onion, finely sliced

½ red chili pepper, finely chopped

2 tablespoons raisins, soaked in a little warm water to soften

3 tablespoons pine nuts

½ tablespoon capers

7 pitted olives, coarsely chopped

1 teaspoon saffron, ground to a powder

14 oz (400 g) *penne* pasta

3–4 tablespoons grated Parmesan, plus extra to serve

sea salt

Cook the cauliflower florets in plenty of boiling water until tender but not mushy, about 5 minutes. Drain and reserve the cooking water.

Meanwhile, heat the olive oil in a large, deep frying pan over medium heat, add the anchovies, and cook until they have melted. Add the onions and chili, and sweat for 1 minute. Add the drained raisins, pine nuts, capers, and olives, and continue to sweat for 1 minute. Add the cooked cauliflower florets and mix well to combine, adding a little salt to taste. Use a little of the cauliflower cooking water to dissolve the saffron powder, then add to the mixture with a further ladleful of cauliflower cooking water. Cover with a lid and continue to cook on a medium–low heat while you cook the pasta.

Bring the cauliflower cooking water back to a boil, adding more water if necessary, and some salt. When boiling, add the pasta and cook until *al dente* (check the instructions on your package for cooking time).

Drain the pasta, reserving a little of the cooking water. Add the pasta to the cauliflower sauce, along with a little of the cooking water, increase the heat, and cook for 2 minutes, or until the pasta has absorbed the liquid. Remove from the heat, stir in the grated Parmesan, and serve immediately, with an extra sprinkling of Parmesan if desired.

MEZZE MANICHE CON BROCCOLI, SPECK E MANDORLE

Mezze Maniche with Broccoli, Speck, and Almonds

Pasta with broccoli is a very common dish in Italy and usually the type of broccoli used is *cime di rape* (broccoli rabe). However, if you can't find it, broccolini or regular broccoli is perfect. For more flavor, I have added *speck*—a smoked air-dried ham—but this can be omitted for vegetarians. The addition of toasted almonds gives the dish a nice crunchy texture. *Mezze maniche* means "short sleeves," referring to the short tubular shape of the pasta. If you can't get this shape, then use *conchiglie* or *penne*.

Serves 4

14 oz (400 g) broccoli rabe, broccolini, or broccoli florets

¼ cup (60 ml) extra-virgin olive oil

5½ oz (150 g) Italian *speck* (smoked air-dried ham), finely chopped

1 garlic clove, finely chopped

1 red chili pepper, finely chopped

11½ oz (325 g) *mezze maniche* pasta

⅓ cup (1½ oz/40 g) whole almonds, toasted and coarsely chopped

⅓ cup (1 oz/30 g) grated Parmesan

sea salt

Bring a large saucepan of salted water to a boil, add the broccoli, and cook for about 10 minutes until tender.

Meanwhile, heat the olive oil in a large frying pan over medium heat, add the *speck,* and sauté for 2 minutes. Add the garlic and chili, and continue to sauté for 1 minute or so.

Using a slotted spoon, remove the broccoli florets from their cooking water and add them to the frying pan. Increase the heat to high and sauté for about 3 minutes. Season with a little salt to taste.

Bring the broccoli cooking water back to a boil, add the *mezze maniche,* and cook until *al dente* (check the instructions on your package for cooking time).

Drain the pasta, reserving a little cooking water. Add the pasta and reserved coooking water to the frying pan with the broccoli sauce and cook over a medium–high heat until well amalgamated.

Remove from the heat, mix in the toasted almonds and grated Parmesan, and serve immediately.

Dried Pasta

GNOCCHETTI SARDI CON SALAME E PESTO DI PISTACCHIO E LIMONE

Gnocchetti Sardi with Salami and a Pistachio and Lemon Pesto

I love pistachioss—combined with fresh Amalfi lemon zest and some parsley, they make a deliciously refreshing pesto sauce. In this recipe, I have combined the pesto with salami to give the dish an extra kick. For maximum flavor, try to use a chunk of salami that you can cut into pieces instead of pre-sliced—you could even ask your deli to cut the salami into small cubes. For vegetarians, simply omit the salami.

Serves 4

11½ oz (325 g) *gnocchetti sardi* pasta

sea salt

3½ oz (100 g) Italian Milano salami, cut into small cubes

For the pesto:

scant ½ cup (1¾ oz/50 g) shelled pistachios

zest of 1 Amalfi lemon or a good-quality unwaxed organic lemon

½ cup (1¾ oz/50 g) grated Parmesan

½ handful of parsley

3 tablespoons extra-virgin olive oil

Bring a large saucepan of salted water to a boil and cook the *gnocchetti sardi* until *al dente* (check the instructions on your package for cooking time).

Meanwhile, put all the pesto ingredients into a food processor and blend until you obtain a fairly smooth but still crunchy consistency. To help it along, trickle in a little of the pasta cooking water (3–4 tablespoons) while the machine is running.

Drain the pasta, combine it with the pesto and the salami cubes, and serve immediately.

MAFALDINE CON RICOTTA

Mafaldine with Ricotta

Pasta with ricotta was always a quick and simple childhood favorite. Ricotta is low in calories, so it's a healthy option too! Try to get the best ricotta you can from a good Italian deli. *Mafaldine* pasta is a *tagliatelle*-type shape with a curly edge, which is ideal with this creamy ricotta sauce. If you can't find *mafaldine*, you could substitute with *farfalle* or *linguine*.

Serves 4

11½ oz (325 g) *mafaldine* pasta

¼ cup (60 ml) extra-virgin olive oil

pat of butter

5 sage leaves

3 onions, very finely chopped

1½ cups (12 oz/350 g) ricotta

scant ½ cup (1½ oz/40 g) grated pecorino or Parmesan

sea salt and freshly ground black pepper

Bring a large saucepan of salted water to a boil and cook the *mafaldine* until *al dente* (check the instructions on your package for cooking time).

Meanwhile, heat the olive oil and butter in a large frying pan over medium heat, add the sage leaves and onions, and sauté for about 7 minutes, stirring from time to time to avoid sticking or burning. Stir in the ricotta with 4 tablespoons of the pasta cooking water and mix together well until you obtain a creamy consistency. Season with salt and pepper to taste.

Drain the pasta and add it to the sauce, along with half of the grated pecorino or Parmesan. Cook for about 1 minute, adding a little more of the pasta water if necessary.

Remove from the heat and serve immediately, sprinkled with the remaining grated cheese and some more freshly ground black pepper.

PENNETTE CON LENTICCHIE E FUNGHI

Pennette with Lentils and Mushrooms

Pasta with lentils is a very common dish throughout Italy and made in a variety of ways. It's quick, easy, and makes a nutritious meal at any time. This particular dish has the addition of mushrooms—I have opted for cremini mushrooms, but you could add whichever variety you prefer; during fall, you could even treat yourself to delicious porcini! The best lentils in Italy are from Castelluccio, obtainable from good Italian delis. Alternatively, you can use the small brown or French green varieties, which are widely available. You don't normally need to pre-soak them, although always check your package for cooking instructions.

Serves 4

1 cup (7 oz/200 g) Castelluccio lentils
 (alternatively, use green or brown lentils)

10½ oz (300 g) *pennette* pasta

¼ cup (60 ml) extra-virgin oilve oil

2 garlic cloves, peeled and left whole

5¾ oz (160 g) cremini mushrooms,
 thinly sliced

scant 1 cup (7 oz/200 g) tomato passata
 (strained tomato purée)

3 tablespoons grated Parmesan

sea salt

a little finely chopped parsley, to serve

Cook the lentils in boiling water until tender (check the instructions on your package for cooking time).

Meanwhile, bring another large saucepan of salted water to a boil and cook the pasta until *al dente* (check the instructions on your package for cooking time).

At the same time, heat the olive oil in a frying pan over medium heat, add the garlic cloves, and sweat for 1 minute. Add the mushrooms and fry, stirring, for 5 minutes, then add the passata and cook for 10 minutes. Drain the cooked lentils and add to the tomato sauce.

Drain the pasta, add it to the sauce, and mix to combine. Mix in the grated Parmesan, then remove from the heat and serve, sprinkled with a little chopped parsley.

FUSILLI INTEGRALI CON SALSA ALLA CRUDAIOLA

Wholewheat Fusilli with Fresh Tomatoes

This is a perfect uncomplicated dish for those hot summer days when you don't feel like cooking much and tomatoes are at their best. The sauce can be made in advance and the only thing you need to cook is the pasta. Healthy wholewheat *fusilli* works really well, but you could also use ordinary *fusilli*. I love a sprinkling of salted ricotta on top. If you prefer, you can omit the onions and simply add more tomatoes.

Serves 4

10½ oz (300 g) baby plum tomatoes, halved and deseeded

2 red *cipolotti* (large scallions) or 1 small red onion, finely sliced

a handful of basil leaves

1 teaspoon dried oregano

1 red chili pepper, finely sliced

¼ cup (60 ml) extra-virgin olive oil

11½ oz (325 g) wholewheat *fusilli* pasta

sea salt

ricotta salata, grated or crumbled, to serve (optional)

In a large bowl, combine the tomatoes, onions, basil, dried oregano, chilli, olive oil, and salt to taste. Cover with plastic wrap and leave to marinate for about 1 hour.

Bring a large saucepan of salted water to a boil and cook the *fusilli* until al dente (check the instructions on your package for cooking time). Drain the pasta well and combine with the tomato mixture.

Serve, sprinkled with some *ricotta salata* if desired.

LINGUINE AL LIMONE

Linguine with Lemon

This quick and light dish is perfect for summer. It is very popular on the Amalfi Coast, where the lemons are exquisite! When making this dish, please do use the very best lemons you can find.

Serves 4

12 oz (350 g) *linguine* pasta

3 tablespoons (1½ oz/40 g) butter

1 tablespoon extra-virgin olive oil

1 garlic clove, left whole

zest and juice of 1 large unwaxed organic lemon (preferably Amalfi lemon)

2 tablespoons chopped parsley

sea salt

Bring a large saucepan of salted water to a boil and cook the *linguine* until *al dente* (check the instructions on your package for cooking time).

Heat the butter and olive oil in a frying pan over medium heat, add the garlic, and sauté for 1 minute or so until it begins to change color, then remove and discard the garlic. Add the lemon zest and juice to the pan.

Drain the *linguine*, add it to the pan, along with the parsley, and mix well. Remove from the heat and serve immediately.

Dried Pasta

SPIRALI CON PESTO DI AGRUMI

Spirali with Citrus Pesto

This Sicilian-inspired pesto is quick to prepare, refreshing, and delicious, and can also be eaten cold, so leftovers are perfect for your lunchbox the next day. It makes a delicious topping for crostini, too, so it's worth making plenty. You can store it in the refrigerator for a few days or freeze to use at another time.

Serves 4

2 oranges

2 tablespoons capers

1 teaspoon dried oregano

1 garlic clove, peeled and left whole

11½ oz (325 g) *spirali* pasta

a large handful of basil leaves

⅓ cup (1¾ oz/50 g) blanched almonds

scant ½ cup (1¾ oz/50 g) shelled pistachios

2 tablespoons extra-virgin olive oil

sea salt

zest of 1 lemon, to serve

Zest one of the oranges and set aside the zest. Peel both oranges.

Using a sharp knife, segment the peeled oranges by cutting between the segment walls, discarding the pith but keeping any juice that collects. Put the segments and juice into a large bowl. Add the capers, oregano, garlic, and a pinch of salt; stir to combine, and leave to infuse for about 10 minutes while you prepare the other ingredients.

Bring a large saucepan of salted water to a boil and cook the *spirali* until *al dente* (check the instructions on your package for cooking time).

Put the basil leaves, almonds, pistachios, olive oil, and the infused orange mixture into a food processor and process until smooth and creamy.

Drain the *spirali*, mix with the citrus pesto, and sprinkle with the orange and lemon zest. Serve immediately,

CASARECCE ALLA NERANO

Casarecce with Zucchini and Provolone

This is my own version of this classic recipe from the Campania region. First made in the coastal town of Nerano, it is usually made with *spaghetti* and *Provolone del Monaco*, an aged cheese from the Monti Lattari, the mountainous area inland from the Amalfi Coast. If you are lucky enough to find this cheese in a good Italian deli, or bring some back from a trip to the region, try it in this recipe. Otherwise, a *provolone piccante* will work just as well.

Serves 4

vegetable or sunflower oil, for deep-frying

3 zucchini (about 1 lb 7 oz/650 g), thinly sliced into rounds

a handful of fresh basil leaves, torn

11½ oz (325 g) *casarecce* pasta

¼ cup (60 ml) extra-virgin olive oil

1 garlic clove, left whole

scant ½ cup (1½ oz/40 g) grated Parmesan

5½ oz (150 g) *provolone piccante*, 4½ oz (120 g) grated; 1 oz (30 g) shaved

sea salt and freshly ground black pepper

In a deep heavy saucepan, heat enough oil for deep-frying. Working in batches, deep-fry the zucchini slices in the hot oil for a couple of minutes until golden. Using a slotted spoon, transfer the fried zucchini to a plate lined with paper towels to drain, laying them flat in a single layer. Sprinkle with salt and a few of the torn basil leaves.

Meanwhile, bring a large saucepan of salted water to a boil and cook the *casarecce* until *al dente* (check the instructions on your package for cooking time).

In a large frying pan, heat the olive oil over medium heat. Add the garlic and sauté for 2 minutes. Remove the garlic, add the fried zucchini, and sauté for 1 minute. Drain the *casarecce*, reserving some of the cooking water. Add the *casarecce*, Parmesan, grated *provolone piccante,* and the remaining basil leaves to the pan with the zucchini and a little of the cooking water; mix to a creamy consistency. Season with black pepper, then remove from the heat.

Serve immediately, topped with the *provolone piccante* shavings.

SPAGHETTI CON CIPOLLE ARROSTITE

Spaghetti with Roasted Onions

Roasted onions have a lovely flavor and are perfect combined with crispy pancetta and tossed with freshly cooked *spaghetti*. If you can cook over charcoal or using a wood-fired oven, the onions will taste even better!

Serves 4

3 red onions

11½ oz (325 g) *spaghetti* pasta

¼ cup (60 ml) extra-virgin olive oil, plus extra for drizzling

7 oz (200 g) pancetta, cubed

⅓ cup (80 ml) white wine

1 teaspoon fennel seeds

sea salt and freshly ground black pepper

Preheat the oven to 400°F (200°C).

Wrap each onion in aluminum foil, place on a baking sheet, and roast for 50 minutes, until cooked through. Remove from the oven and, when cool enough to handle, slice each onion into about 6 wedges. Set aside.

Bring a large saucepan of salted water to a boil and cook the pasta until *al dente* (check the instructions on your package for cooking time).

Meanwhile, heat the olive oil in a frying pan over medium–high heat, add the pancetta, and sauté for about 7 minutes until crispy. Increase the heat, add the white wine, and allow to evaporate by half. Then stir in the roasted onion wedges and fennel seeds.

Drain the *spaghetti*, add it to the sauce, and cook together for 1 minute. Remove from the heat and serve immediately, with some freshly ground black pepper and a drizzle of extra-virgin olive oil.

Well before dried pasta became a global industry, this Italian staple came to us in fresh form from the humble kitchens of *nonnas* and *mammas* all over Italy. Certain shapes are still made by hand today in many towns and villages. If you go to Bari in southern Italy, you can find old ladies making *orecchiette* and *cavatelli* in their own kitchens and selling them to passers-by. They really have quite incredible businesses going and it is fascinating to see how pasta was originally made. It's good fun—if you're lucky, they may even invite you to give it a try yourself!

Contrary to what most people think, fresh pasta is actually quick to make, does not need many ingredients, and is extremely good value. It can be made with eggs or with water and, by using the appropriate flours, there are even some excellent gluten-free varieties. Fresh pasta takes less time to cook than dried pasta— anything from 1 minute for thin *spaghetti* shapes, to about 6 minutes for thicker shapes and filled pasta.

There are all sorts of regional varieties and each town, village, and family have their own specialties. Egg pasta is more common in northern Italy; in areas such as Emilia Romagna it is made for their regional dishes of *lasagne*, *tortellini,* and *tagliatelle*. Eggless pasta, with more bite to it, is more common in southern Italy, and you find varieties such as *orecchiette* in Puglia or *ricci* (a type of *fusilli*) from my home town of Minori. I have fond memories of my Aunt Antonietta who, not so long ago, was still making *ricci* at home when she was well into her nineties.

Of course, if you don't have time to make your own fresh pasta, there are many available to buy. Check out your local Italian deli or supermarket—they now have so many varieties to choose from. And please bear in mind that, in most of the recipes in this chapter, the fresh pasta can be substituted with dried pasta.

FRESH PASTA

TIPS FOR MAKING PERFECT FRESH PASTA

Always use good-quality Italian "00" pasta flour; it's finer than other flours and you will find it easier to work with when making the pasta dough. If you are adding semolina flour to your dough, try to get fine semolina flour, ideally the Italian durum wheat variety known as *semola rimacinata di grano duro*. I highly recommend you get both flours from your nearest Italian deli for the best Italian quality.

When making egg pasta, always use the best free-range organic eggs you can find, with rich yellow yolks.

Eggless pasta is made using just lukewarm water. If you find you need a little more liquid when mixing either type of dough, simply add a little lukewarm water.

Once the dough is made, wrap it tightly in plastic wrap and let it rest for at least 30 minutes in the refrigerator before using. Pasta dough should always be wrapped in plastic when you are not using it. Cover rolled-out pasta sheets and shapes with a damp dish towel to stop them drying out, unless you are using them immediately.

EQUIPMENT FOR MAKING FRESH PASTA

ROLLING PIN Years ago, and certainly when my mom made pasta, she didn't have the luxury of a pasta machine, and instead relied on her trusty rolling pin. So, a rolling pin is always my number one piece of equipment, and I still use one if I'm making just a small quantity of fresh pasta. You have to keep rolling and rolling until you get the desired thickness, but I think of it as a bit of a workout!

PASTA MACHINE This really is a great investment and does cut out a lot of work. Set the machine up on a clean, sturdy work surface and clamp it securely. Click the machine through to its highest setting. Flatten a piece of dough with your hands, feed it between the rollers, and crank the machine to roll it through. Reduce the thickness setting and feed the same piece of dough through again. Keep doing this, reducing the thickness settings as you go, and you will see how much thinner the dough becomes. Finish rolling on setting no. 1 (unless your recipe specifies otherwise), which is usually the narrowest setting, for wafer-thin dough that is suitable for most fresh pasta

shapes and for filled pasta. Your pasta machine will also have attachments for long shapes such as *spaghetti*, *tagliatelle*, *linguine*, or *tagliolini*. Although more expensive, you can also buy an electric machine that mixes the dough for you and comes with attachments for short-shaped pasta too, so you can make your own *penne* as well as *spaghetti*.

PASTA CUTTERS You can buy a lovely variety of round and square pasta cutters in different sizes, but you can also use regular cookie cutters for making filled pasta. A wheel cutter is also nice to have, since it neatens up the rough edges, but you can use a sharp knife instead.

PASTRY BRUSH Very handy when making filled pasta, to brush the edges of the dough with egg wash or water to help them stick together.

EGG PASTA DOUGH

Makes enough to serve 4

generous 1½ cups (7 oz/200 g) Italian "00" pasta flour, sifted

2 extra-large free-range organic eggs

Put the flour into a large mixing bowl or heap on a clean work surface. Make a well in the center, add the eggs, and mix well to form a dough. Wrap in plastic wrap and chill in the refrigerator for 30 minutes, or until required.

EGGLESS PASTA DOUGH

Makes enough to serve 4

generous 1½ cups (7 oz/200 g) Italian "00" pasta flour, sifted

5–7 tablespoons lukewarm water

Use the same method as above, but substitute the eggs with lukewarm water, adding it gradually, since you may need less or a little more.

GLUTEN-FREE PASTA DOUGH

Makes enough to serve 4

1¼ cups (5½ oz/150 g)
   buckwheat flour, sifted

⅓ cup (1¾ oz/50 g) rice flour, sifted,
   plus (optional) extra for dusting

2 eggs

1½ teaspoon extra-virgin olive oil

about 1 tablespoon water

In a large bowl, or on a clean work surface, combine the flours. Make a well in the center, add the eggs and olive oil, and mix, gradually adding the water to make a soft dough (you may need a little more water). Form into a ball, wrap in plastic, and chill in the refrigerator for at least 30 minutes.

Unwrap the chilled dough, divide into 3 or 4 portions, and run through the pasta machine at the highest setting. Keep feeding the dough through, gradually working your way down through the settings to number 4, about ⅛ in (3 mm). Don't go any thinner or the pasta dough will break.

Alternatively, lightly dust a work surface with a little rice flour and roll out the dough to a thickness of ⅛ in (3 mm) using a rolling pin.

Cut the pasta dough into strips or sheets according to your requirements.

GLUTEN-FREE EGGLESS PASTA DOUGH

Makes enough to serve 4

⅔ cup (3½ oz/100 g) rice flour, sifted, plus (optional) extra for dusting

¾ cup (3½ oz/100 g) buckwheat flour, sifted

½ cup (1¾ oz/50 g) chickpea flour (besan), sifted

1½ teaspoons extra-virgin olive oil

about ⅔ cup (150 ml) water

In a large bowl, or on a clean work surface, combine the flours. Make a well in the center, add the olive oil, and mix, gradually adding the water to make a soft dough. Form into a ball, wrap in plastic, and chill in the refrigerator for at least 30 minutes.

Unwrap the chilled dough, divide into 3 or 4 portions, and run through the pasta machine at the highest setting. Keep feeding the dough through, gradually working your way down through the settings to number 4, about ⅛ in (3 mm).

Alternatively, lightly dust a work surface with a little rice flour and roll out the dough to a thickness of ⅛ in (3 mm) using a rolling pin.

Cut the pasta dough into strips or sheets according to your requirements.

PAPPARDELLE CON RAGU DI FUNGHI MISTI

Pappardelle with Mixed Mushroom Ragù

This is a must during the fall, when wild mushrooms are in abundance.
The mushrooms are cooked like a traditional meat ragù and this dish makes
a perfect vegetarian meal. If you can't find wild mushrooms, use a variety
of cultivated ones, which are now easily obtainable all year round.

Serves 4

¼ cup (60 ml) extra-virgin olive oil

1 onion, finely chopped

1 celery stalk, finely chopped

1 carrot, finely chopped

1 garlic clove, finely chopped

½ red chili pepper, finely chopped

2 fresh thyme sprigs

¾ oz (20 g) dried porcini, reconstituted
    in a little warm water

1 lb 2 oz (500 g) mixed wild or cultivated
    mushrooms, cleaned and coarsely chopped

3 tablespoons white wine

1 x 14 oz (400 g) can of chopped plum
    tomatoes

1¼ cups (300 ml) hot vegetable stock

12 oz (350 g) fresh *pappardelle* pasta

sea salt and freshly ground black pepper

grated Parmesan and fresh thyme
    leaves, to serve

Heat the olive oil in a large frying pan over
medium heat. Add the onion, celery, carrot,
garlic, chili, and thyme, and sauté for about
5 minutes until softened. Squeeze out the
soaked dried porcini (reserve the soaking
water) and stir into the pan. Add the fresh
mushrooms and sauté for 1 minute or so.
Increase the heat, add the white wine, and
allow to evaporate. Add the tomatoes, the
reserved porcini soaking water, and the stock,
and season with some salt and pepper. Bring to
a boil, then lower the heat, partially cover with
a lid, and cook gently for 45 minutes.

Just before the mushroom ragù is ready,
bring a large saucepan of salted water to a boil
and cook the *pappardelle* pasta until *al dente*,
2–3 minutes.

Drain the pasta and combine well with the
ragù. Serve immediately with a sprinkling of
grated Parmesan and some fresh thyme.

Fresh Pasta

ROTOLINI DI PASTA RIPIENI CON RADICCHIO E SERVITI CON FONDUTA

Radicchio-Filled Pasta Rolls with Fontina Sauce

This takes a little time to make, but is well worth the effort. The slightly bitter taste of radicchio perfectly complements the rich cheesy sauce. Fontina is ideal for this, but if you can't find it, then a mature Cheddar is perfect!

Serves 6 (makes 2 mini rolls)

1 quantity of Egg Pasta Dough
(see page 79)

For the filling:

3 tablespoons extra-virgin olive oil

3½ oz (100 g) smoked pancetta, finely chopped

1 banana shallot, finely chopped

1 lb 5 oz (600 g) radicchio, finely sliced

leaves of 2 thyme sprigs

⅓ cup (80 ml) red wine

½ cup (1¾ oz/50 g) grated Parmesan

1 egg, beaten

For the fontina sauce:

scant 1 cup (200 ml) light cream

5½ oz (150 g) fontina, chopped into small cubes or grated

freshly ground black pepper

Make the pasta dough as described on page 79.

Heat the olive oil in a large saucepan over medium heat, add the pancetta and shallot, and sweat for 2 minutes. Increase the heat to medium–high, add the radicchio and thyme, and sauté for 2 minutes. Add the wine and allow to evaporate, then reduce the heat, cover, and cook gently for 10–15 minutes, until the radicchio has softened. Remove from the heat, let cool slightly, then mix in half of the Parmesan.

Divide the pasta dough into 2 equal pieces. Roll each piece to a thin rectangle, about 14 x 9½ in (36 x 24 cm), and carefully place each rectangle on a separate clean dish towel. Evenly spoon over the filling, dividing it equally, leaving a 2 in (5 cm) border all around. Sprinkle the remaining Parmesan over the filling and brush the edges with beaten egg. Use the dish towels to carefully roll up the dough from the longer sides, like a jelly roll, pressing the final edges to seal them, and folding up the ends. Roll up in the dish towels, twisting the ends like a candy wrapper, and secure with some kitchen twine.

Half-fill a large deep pan (I use a flame-safe roasting pan) with water and bring to a boil over medium–high heat. Place the 2 *rotoli* inside, adding more boiling water from the kettle if necessary, so that they are completely submerged, and cook at a rapid simmer for 30 minutes.

Meanwhile, make the sauce: put the cream and fontina into a bain-marie, or a bowl set over a pan of simmering water, and stir with a wooden spoon until the cheese melts. Season with black pepper.

Carefully remove the *rotoli* from the water, unwrap, trim, and discard the ends, then slice into rounds and serve with the fontina sauce.

LAGANE E CECI

Lagane with Chickpeas

Halfway between a soup and *pastasciutta* (pasta dishes that are not soupy), this ancient traditional recipe is comfort food at its best. Made with a few basic ingredients and popular in the southern Italian regions of Campania, Basilicata, and Calabria, it is said to be one of the oldest pasta dishes there is. The shape, cut into short wide ribbons, is said to have influenced *lasagne*, hence its name: *lagane*. If you have time, you can of course use dried chickpeas rather than canned—check the package for how long they need to soak and pre-cook before proceeding as below.

Serves 4

1 quantity of Eggless Pasta Dough
  (see page 79)

¼ cup (60 ml) extra-virgin olive oil

2 garlic cloves

5½ oz (150 g) *guanciale* (cured pork cheek) or
  smoked pancetta, cut into small cubes

2 rosemary sprigs

2 x 14 oz (400 g) cans of chickpeas, drained

6⅓ cups (1.5 liters) hot vegetable stock

scant ½ cup (1½ oz/40 g) grated pecorino

a handful of parsley, finely chopped

Italian "00" pasta flour, for dusting

Make the pasta dough as described on page 79.

Heat the olive oil in a large saucepan over medium heat. Add the garlic, pancetta, and rosemary, and sweat for about 3 minutes. Add the chickpeas and sauté for 1 minute, then add the vegetable stock and continue to cook for about 5 minutes.

Meanwhile, roll out the pasta dough on a lightly floured work surface to a thickness of ¼ in (5 mm). Cut the dough into ribbons about 1½ x 3 in (4 x 8 cm).

Add the pasta ribbons (*lagane*) to the pan and cook for 7–8 minutes, until the *lagane* are cooked *al dente*.

Remove from the heat, stir in the grated pecorino and the parsley, and serve immediately.

PASTA E FAGIOLI DI ADRIANA

Adriana's Pasta and Beans

Pasta e fagioli were and still are a favorite comfort food in my family. There are many variations and recipes differ, not only from region to region, but also among families—there are always disputes on how to make the best version. This is my sister Adriana's recipe. You can make it with more liquid by adding more stock, but according to Adriana the real *pasta e fagioli* should have a thicker consistency. Well, I'm not going to argue because it is delicious and I always have seconds! If you don't have fresh pasta, you can make it with the dried variety, too. Time permitting, you could use dried borlotti beans if you prefer—just check the soaking and cooking times on the package.

Serves 4

¼ cup (60 ml) extra-virgin olive oil, plus extra for drizzling

3½ oz (100 g) pancetta, diced

1 onion, finely sliced

1 celery stalk, finely sliced, plus a few reserved celery leaves

1 garlic clove, left whole

1 rosemary sprig

2 x 14 oz (400 g) cans of borlotti beans, drained

6⅓ cups (1.5 liters) hot vegetable stock

9 oz (250 g) fresh pasta, such as *tagliatelle* or *pappardelle*, roughly cut into 3 in (8 cm) lengths

sea salt and freshly ground black pepper

Heat the olive oil in a large saucepan over medium heat, add the pancetta, and sauté for 1 minute. Add the onion, celery, garlic, and rosemary, and sauté for 2 minutes. Stir in the borlotti beans, add the vegetable stock, and bring to a boil. Then reduce the heat, cover with a lid, and cook gently for 20 minutes.

Remove about a quarter of the beans and blend in a food processor to a fairly smooth consistency. Set aside.

Increase the heat, add the fresh pasta to the pot, along with the celery leaves, and cook for about 2 minutes, until the pasta is *al dente*.

Remove from the heat and stir in the mashed beans. Taste for seasoning and add a little salt if necessary; then cover with a lid and let rest for 5 minutes. Serve with a sprinkling of black pepper and a drizzle of extra-virgin olive oil.

ORECCHIETTE FRESCHE AL POMODORO CON BURRATA AL LIMONE

Fresh Orecchiette with Tomatoes and Lemon Burrata

Orecchiette (literally "little ears") originate from Puglia in southern Italy, where it is not uncommon to see ladies outside their houses making this traditional eggless pasta. Local restaurant menus serve freshly made *orecchiette* with *cime di rape* (broccoli rabe), with meat ragù, or simply with a delicious fresh tomato sauce, as here. To finish, I have added burrata, a soft, creamy buffalo-milk cheese from Puglia, and a sprinkling of lemon zest for a refreshing taste. If you can't get *burrata*, use buffalo mozzarella. If you want to make your own *orecchiette*, use the Eggless Pasta recipe on page 79. Otherwise, they can be bought in good Italian delis.

Serves 4

2 tablespoons extra-virgin olive oil

1 small onion, very finely chopped

11½ oz (325 g) baby plum tomatoes, halved

a handful of basil leaves

14 oz (400 g) fresh *orecchiette* pasta (store-bought or see Eggless Pasta recipe on page 79)

⅓ cup (1 oz/30 g) grated Parmesan

9 oz (250 g) burrata, roughly torn

zest of 1 small unwaxed organic lemon

sea salt and freshly ground black pepper

Heat the olive oil in a frying pan over medium heat, add the onion, and sauté for 2 minutes. Add the tomatoes and basil leaves, season with a little salt, and cook for 10 minutes, stirring with a wooden spoon from time to time.

Meanwhile, bring a large saucepan of salted water to a boil and cook the *orecchiette* until *al dente*, about 5 minutes.

Drain the pasta and add it to the tomato sauce, along with the grated Parmesan. Mix well, then remove from the heat.

Serve immediately with the burrata, lemon zest, and a sprinkling of black pepper.

PIZZOCCHERI VALTELLINESI

Buckwheat Pasta with Savoy Cabbage and Taleggio

This robust mountain dish from the northern region of Valtellina is comfort food at its best, especially during colder months. This nutritious vegetarian dish has ancient roots—buckwheat has long been an important grain grown in this area, and pasta and many other dishes are made from it. Locally grown ingredients such as potatoes and cabbage are used to flavor the *pizzoccheri,* as well as cheeses such as Bitto, Asiago Taleggio, or other local varieties. If you don't want to make your own, you can find dried ready-made *pizzoccheri* from good Italian delis. Make sure you have a preheated dish on hand when you're ready to assemble the ingredients.

Serves 6

For the pasta dough:

generous 1½ cups (7 oz/200 g) Italian "00" pasta flour, plus extra for dusting

2½ cups (10½ oz/300 g) buckwheat flour

a pinch of salt

1 cup (250 ml) hot water (not boiling)

For the sauce:

9 oz (250 g) potatoes, peeled and cut into ½ in (1 cm) cubes

3½ cups (9 oz/250 g) finely sliced Savoy cabbage leaves

7 oz (200 g) Taleggio, cut into small cubes

½ cup (1¾ oz/50 g) grated Parmesan

6 tablespoons (3 oz/85 g) butter

2 garlic cloves, left whole and squashed

sea salt and freshly ground black pepper

First, make the pasta dough. In a large bowl or on a clean work surface, combine the flours and salt. Make a well in the middle and gradually pour in the hot water, mixing continuously to form a dough. Knead lightly until you obtain a smooth, soft dough, then form into a ball, wrap in plastic, and leave to rest for at least 30 minutes.

Unwrap the dough and roll out on a lightly floured work surface until it is ¼ in (5 mm) thick. Alternatively, run through a pasta machine, working through the settings until you get to the smallest one. Cut into long *tagliatelle* shapes, then cut them in half to make the *pizzoccheri*.

In a large saucepan of salted water, bring the potatoes and cabbage to a boil and cook for a further 4 minutes. Add the *pizzoccheri* and continue to cook for a couple of minutes, until the pasta is *al dente*.

Meanwhile, preheat a serving dish.

Drain the pasta and vegetables. In the hot serving dish, arrange a layer of *pizzoccheri* and vegetables, and scatter over some Taleggio cubes and grated Parmesan. Continue to make layers in this way until the all the ingredients have been used up.

In a small frying pan, melt the butter. Add the garlic cloves, cook for 1 minute, then remove the garlic and pour the foaming melted butter over the top of the pasta dish. The heat should melt the cheeses slightly. Gently mix well with a fork, then season with salt and pepper, and serve immediately.

TAGLIATELLE FRESCHE CON FUNGHI E ASPARAGI

Fresh Tagliatelle with Mushrooms and Asparagus

I love making this quick and simple dish during spring, when I can forage for mealy edible wild mushrooms, and which usually coincides with the first of the asparagus. Unfortunately, most wild mushroom varieties are not readily available in grocery stores or markets, so please use cultivated white or oyster mushrooms, unless of course you are lucky to find delicious white springtime fungi in meadows and fields. As with all wild mushrooms, please be careful and only pick them if you are absolutely sure they are edible. You can either make the fresh *tagliatelle* yourself (see fresh pasta dough recipes on page 79) or buy ready-made.

Serves 4

6 tablespoons extra-virgin olive oil

4 garlic cloves, finely sliced

½ red chili pepper, finely chopped

10½ oz (300 g) mushrooms, finely sliced

1 cup (5½ oz/150 g) baby plum tomatoes, halved

11½ oz (325 g) fresh *tagliatelle* pasta

5½ oz (150 g) asparagus, finely chopped, keeping tips intact

sea salt

grated Parmesan, to serve (optional)

Bring a large saucepan of salted water to a boil.

Meanwhile, heat the olive oil in a large frying pan over medium heat, add the garlic and chili, and sweat for 1 minute. Add the mushrooms and sauté for 1 minute. Stir in the tomatoes and cook for 1 minute.

At this point, add the *tagliatelle* to the pan of boiling water and cook for 1–2 minutes or until *al dente*.

While the pasta cooks, add the asparagus and some salt to the frying pan, then stir in about ⅔ cup (150 ml) of the hot pasta water. Cover and cook for about 3 minutes.

Drain the *tagliatelle*, add it to the sauce, and mix together over high heat for 1 minute. Remove from the heat and serve with freshly grated Parmesan, if desired.

Fresh Pasta

PISAREI E FASO'

Eggless Pasta Dumplings with Beans

This ancient traditional peasant dish from Emilia Romagna is so delicious that, when I tested the recipe with my family, we realized we had finished it all in no time! It is a popular dish in the Piacenza area, where you can find it in local trattorias as well as quality restaurants. The eggless fresh pasta and simple bean and tomato sauce makes it perfect for vegans.

Serves 4

generous 1½ cups (7 oz/200 g) Italian "00" pasta flour, plus extra for dusting

pinch of sea salt

1⅓ cups (2½ oz/70 g) breadcrumbs

generous ½ cup (140 ml) warm water

For the bean and tomato sauce:

2 tablespoons extra-virgin olive oil

1 onion, finely chopped

2 x 14 oz (400 g) cans of borlotti beans, drained

generous 2 cups (500 ml) tomato passata (strained tomato purée)

sea salt and freshly ground black pepper

In a large bowl or on a clean work surface, combine the flour, salt, and breadcrumbs, then gradually add warm water and mix to form a smooth dough. Wrap in plastic and leave to rest for 30 minutes.

Meanwhile, make the sauce. Heat the olive oil in a saucepan over a medium–low heat, add the onion, and sweat until softened. Add the drained borlotti beans, mix well, and cook for 1 minute. Add the passata and season with salt and pepper. Mix well, cover with a lid, and cook over medium heat for 20 minutes.

Unwrap the dough, cut out a chunk, and roll out into a thin sausage shape on a lightly floured work surface (keep the remaining dough wrapped in plastic until required). Cut the dough into ⅓ in (1 cm) pieces, like little gnocchi, and press each piece with your finger to make a slight indentation. Continue until you have used up all the dough.

Bring a large saucepan of salted water to a boil and add the *pisarei*. Cook until they rise to the top, then cook for a further 2 minutes. Drain with a slotted spoon and add to the sauce, mixing well to combine. Remove from the heat, allow to rest for a minute, then serve.

SCIALATIELLI CON SUGO DI MELANZANE

Scialatielli with Eggplant Sauce

This typical pasta from the Amalfi Coast is a relatively modern recipe, first made in the 1970s by a local chef who added milk, grated cheese, and chopped fresh herbs to the pasta dough. It was a success, and is now a much-loved pasta dish in the Campania region of southern Italy. It is perfectly combined with sauces using local ingredients such as shellfish, lemons, Neapolitan meat ragù, or vegetables such as eggplant, which I have used in this recipe. Alternatively, a simple fresh cherry tomato sauce or butter and lemon are equally delicious.

Serves 4–6

½ cup (125 ml) milk

1 egg

1½ tablespoon extra-virgin olive oil

scant 2½ cups (14 oz/400 g) semolina flour (*semola di grano duro rimaccinata*), plus extra for dusting

⅓ cup (1 oz/30 g) grated pecorino

a handful of basil leaves, finely chopped

For the eggplant sauce:

¼ cup (60 ml) extra-virgin olive oil

1 lb (450 g) eggplant, cut into thin strips

1 garlic clove, left whole and squashed

1 x 14 oz (400 g) can of chopped plum tomatoes

a handful of basil, roughly torn, plus extra to serve

3 tablespoons grated pecorino, plus extra to serve

sea salt and freshly ground black pepper

In a small bowl, combine the milk, egg, and extra-virgin olive oil.

In a large bowl or on a clean work surface, combine the semolina flour, grated pecorino, and chopped basil. Make a well in the middle and gradually pour in the liquid mixture, mixing well to form a soft dough. Wrap in plastic wrap and put into the refrigerator to rest for 30 minutes.

Meanwhile, make the eggplant sauce. Heat the olive oil in a large saucepan over a medium–high heat, add the eggplant strips and fry, stirring, until golden. Remove with tongs and drain on paper towels. In the same pan, sweat the garlic for 1 minute to flavor the oil, then remove it. Add the tomatoes and basil with some salt and pepper, and cook, covered, over medium heat, for 15 minutes, stirring from time to time. Add the fried eggplants and continue to cook for 5 minutes.

Lightly dust a clean work surface with some semolina flour, and roll out the dough to a thickness of ¼ in (5 mm). Cut out strips of dough, about 4½ in (12 cm) in length.

Bring a large saucepan of salted water to a boil, add the *scialatielli* pasta, and cook for about 4 minutes. Drain with a slotted spoon, add it to the eggplant sauce, add the grated pecorino, and mix well to combine over medium–high heat. Remove from the heat and serve immediately, with an extra sprinkling of grated pecorino if desired and a few fresh basil leaves.

Fresh Pasta

TONNARELLI CACIO E PEPE

Tonnarelli with Pecorino Romano and Black Pepper

Tonnarelli are like thick square-cut *spaghetti*, sometimes known as *spaghetti alla chittara* due to the traditional method of making this shape with a gadget resembling guitar strings. *Cacio e Pepe* is a popular Roman recipe using just two additional ingredients: pecorino cheese and black pepper. Try to get Pecorino Romano from an Italian deli for the strong, robust flavor this dish is famous for. Although this is a simple dish to make, you have to work quickly once the pasta starts cooking—the pasta water is used not only to loosen up the pasta to mix with the pepper, but also to melt the cheese, which is mixed separately and added to the pasta once it is removed from the heat to avoid it getting lumpy. This is my version of this traditional recipe, however you can use more or less pepper and cheese according to taste. If you don't want to make your own *tonnarelli*, you could use fresh or dried thick *spaghetti*.

Serves 4

11½ oz (325 g) fresh thick *spaghetti*
   or *tonnarelli* pasta

or

1 quantity of Egg Pasta Dough
   (see page 79)

2 tablespoons black peppercorns

5¾ oz (160 g) Pecorino Romano, very finely
   grated, plus extra for sprinkling

sea salt and freshly ground black pepper

If making your own pasta, make the pasta dough as described on page 79. Roll the pasta dough out to a thickness of about ⅛ in (3 mm) or to setting number 4 of your pasta machine. Feed the dough through the thick *spaghetti* attachment for your pasta machine. Cover the pasta with a damp dish towel and set aside while you make the sauce.

Heat a large dry frying pan over high heat and briefly toast the peppercorns. Transfer the peppercorns to a mortar and pestle and crush until fine. Put the crushed pepper back into the frying pan, but keep off the heat.

Put the pecorino cheese into a bowl and set aside.

Bring a large saucepan of salted water to a boil, add the *tonnarelli* pasta, and cook for just under 2 minutes, until *al dente*. As the pasta begins to cook, scoop out a ladleful of the pasta water and add to the frying pan with the pepper, set over medium heat.

Spoon another couple of ladlefuls of pasta water into the bowl with the pecorino, stirring well until you obtain a creamy mixture.

When the pasta is cooked, use a pair of tongs to transfer it to the frying pan. Increase the heat to high and cook for 1 minute.

Remove the frying pan from the heat, add the cheesy mixture to the pasta, and mix until well combined. Serve immediately with a sprinkling of grated pecorino and some more ground black pepper.

LINGUINE CON TONNO FRESCO E BRICIOLE

Linguine with Fresh Tuna and a Breadcrumb Topping

This is quick and easy to make and uses nutritious fresh tuna. The crunchy topping of toasted breadcrumbs and pine nuts adds texture to this light, healthy dish. Buy ready-made fresh *linguine* from your Italian deli or supermarket, or make your own.

Serves 4

14 oz (400 g) fresh *linguine* pasta (store-bought, or see the Egg Pasta recipe or the Eggless Pasta recipe on page 79)

¼ cup (60 ml) extra-virgin olive oil

2 banana shallots, finely chopped

1 lb 2 oz (500 g) fresh tuna, cut into chunks

grated zest of ½ lemon

scant ½ cup (100 ml) white wine

a handful of parsley, finely chopped

¾ cup (1½ oz/40 g) fresh wholewheat breadcrumbs, toasted

2 tablespoons pine nuts, toasted

sea salt and freshly ground black pepper

If making your own pasta, make the dough according to the instructions on page 79. After rolling out to ¼ in (5 mm) in a pasta machine, run it through the *linguine* attachment.

Bring a large saucepan of salted water to a boil and cook the fresh pasta until *al dente*, 1–2 minutes.

Meanwhile, heat the olive oil in a large frying pan, add the shallots, and sauté over medium heat until softened. Increase the heat, add the tuna chunks, season with salt and pepper, and sauté until seared on all sides. Add the lemon zest and white wine, and allow to evaporate.

Drain the pasta and add it to the pan, then stir in the parsley. Mix well together over medium heat for 1 minute.

Remove from the heat and serve immediately, topped with toasted breadcrumbs and pine nuts.

TAGLIERINI AL NERO DI SEPPIA CON CAPESANTE

Squid Ink Taglierini with Scallops

For seafood lovers, this recipe is a must. The pasta dough is flavored with squid ink, turning it a lovely black color, and it combines perfectly with the delicate, tender scallops. If you want to make your own fresh pasta, good Italian delis will stock sachets of squid ink. Alternatively, you can buy ready-made fresh or dried squid ink pasta, such as *spaghetti*, *linguine*, *taglierini*, *tagliolini*, or *capelli d'angelo*. The latter three shapes are all long pasta ribbons, about ¹⁄₁₆ in (2 mm) wide, which are perfect for this sophisticated seafood dish.

Serves 4

12 oz (350 g) fresh squid ink *taglierini* or *spaghetti* pasta

or

1 quantity of Egg Pasta Dough (see page 79)

1 x ⅛ oz (4 g) sachet squid ink

¼ cup (60 ml) extra-virgin olive oil, plus extra for drizzling

4 garlic cloves, finely sliced

½ red chili pepper, finely sliced

8 large shucked scallops, roe separated, white flesh cut lengthways into 3 or 4 slices

8 anchovy fillets

1 tablespoon capers

scant ½ cup (100 ml) white wine

a handful of parsley, finely chopped

6 cherry tomatoes, thinly sliced

sea salt

If making your own squid ink *taglierini*, make the pasta dough as described on page 79, adding the squid ink with the eggs. Mix well to achieve a soft black pasta dough. To make the *taglierini* shape, roll up the pasta sheet and slice into ribbons, ¹⁄₁₆–⅛ in (2–3 mm) wide.

Bring a large saucepan of salted water to a boil.

Meanwhile, heat the olive oil in a large frying pan over medium heat, add the garlic and chili, and sweat for 1 minute. Add the scallop roe, anchovy fillets, and capers, and sweat for a few seconds, then stir in the scallop slices. Increase the heat, add the white wine, and allow to evaporate.

Add the pasta to the saucepan of boiling water and cook for about 1 minute, until *al dente*. Using a pair of tongs, lift the pasta out of the water and add it to the scallop sauce, mixing over high heat until well combined. Season with some salt and stir in the parsley and tomatoes. Serve immediately with a drizzle of extra-virgin olive oil.

BIGOLI ALLA VENETA

Bigoli with Anchovy and Onion Sauce

Bigoli are thick *spaghetti*-type pasta shapes with a rough surface. They are enjoyed in Venice and the Veneto region, where you can find them ready-made either fresh or dried. If you don't have a *bigoli* extruder for your pasta machine, you can simply make thicker *spaghetti*. This simple sauce was traditionally made during times such as Lent or on Fridays, when meat was forbidden.

Serves 4

1 quantity of Eggless Pasta Dough
   (see page 79)
Italian "00" pasta flour, for dusting

For the sauce:

3 tablespoons extra-virgin olive oil
2 onions, finely sliced
12 anchovy fillets
2 tablespoons white wine
sea salt and freshly ground black pepper

Make the pasta dough as described on page 79.

Roll out the pasta and run through the *bigoli* extruder on a pasta machine. Alternatively, roll out using a rolling pin to a thickness of ¼ in (5 mm) on a lightly floured surface, and cut into thick *spaghetti*.

To make the sauce, heat the olive oil in a non-stick saucepan over low–medium heat, add the onions and anchovy fillets, and sweat until the onions become translucent. Add the white wine, cover, and gently cook for about 20 minutes, stirring from time to time.

Meanwhile, bring a large saucepan of salted water to a boil, add the *bigoli* pasta, and cook for about 4 minutes, until *al dente*.

Drain the *bigoli*, add to it the sauce, then increase the heat and mix together for about 1 minute, until well combined. Remove from the heat and check for seasoning, adding a little salt if necessary and a good sprinkling of black pepper. Serve immediately.

QUADRUCCI AL BRODO DI POLLO

Quadrucci in Chicken Broth

This is every Italian's childhood comfort food—a delicate homemade chicken broth with small pasta shapes. You could make your own *quadrucci* (small squares) with the Egg Pasta Dough on page 79, shaped into *tagliatelle* then cut into ½ in (1 cm) squares, or simply buy ready-made fresh *tagliatelle* and cut it up. Try to get the best chicken you can afford—if you like, you could add a store-bought chicken stock gel pot while the broth is cooking, for maximum flavor. If you do this, you will not need to add salt. You can also serve the broth as an appetizer and enjoy the chicken and vegetables as a main course.

Serves 4–6

9 oz (250 g) *quadrucci* pasta, or fresh *tagliatelle* pasta cut into ½ in (1 cm) squares

grated Parmesan, to serve (optional)

For the broth:

2 lb 12 oz (1.2 kg) whole chicken

1 large onion, halved

2 celery stalks with leaves, halved

2 carrots, chopped into large chunks

a handful of flat-leaf parsley

1 teaspoon sea salt

4 black peppercorns

Put all the broth ingredients into a large heavy stockpot, along with enough water to cover the chicken (about 12⅔ cups/3 liters). Bring to a boil, then reduce the heat to low, cover, and simmer gently for about 1½ hours.

Remove the cooked chicken and vegetables from the pot and set aside. Strain the liquid through a fine sieve set over a bowl to obtain a clear broth. Taste for seasoning and, if necessary, add a little more salt. Return the broth to the pot and bring back to a boil, then add the *quadrucci* and cook for 1–2 minutes, or until *al dente*.

Remove from the heat, divide among individual soup bowls, and serve with a sprinkling of grated Parmesan, if desired. Serve the chicken and vegetables as a main course, or as a separate meal.

TAGLIATELLE AL RAGU DI STINCO D'AGNELLO

Tagliatelle with Lamb Shank Ragù

Here, lamb shank is slow-cooked to give a rich-tasting ragù that combines perfectly with fresh egg *tagliatelle*. After cooking, the meat easily comes off the bone to be eaten with the sauce and pasta. Either make your own fresh *tagliatelle* using the Egg Pasta Dough recipe on page 79 or buy it ready-made.

Serves 4

2 tablespoons extra-virgin olive oil

1 lamb shank (about 14 oz/400 g)

1 rosemary sprig

½ small onion, finely chopped

½ celery stalk, finely chopped

1 small carrot, finely chopped

1 tablespoon tomato paste stirred into
2 tablespoons red wine

2 x 14 oz (400 g) cans of chopped
plum tomatoes

14 oz (400 g) fresh *tagliatelle* pasta

sea salt and freshly ground black pepper

grated Parmesan, to serve

Heat the olive oil in a medium saucepan over medium heat, add the lamb shank, and sear well all over, then remove and set aside. To the same pan, add the rosemary sprig and vegetables, and sweat for a couple of minutes, then return the lamb to the pan, and season with salt and pepper. Stir in the tomato paste mixture and the chopped tomatoes, along with half a tomato can of water. Bring to a boil, then reduce the heat, cover, and cook gently for 2½ hours.

Remove the lamb shank and take the meat off the bone, discarding the bone. Break the meat into small pieces and set aside.

Bring a large saucepan of salted water to a boil and cook the *tagliatelle* for 1–2 minutes or until *al dente*. Drain the pasta, then combine with the tomato ragù. Serve with the pieces of lamb and some freshly grated Parmesan.

TONNARELLI CON SALSICCIA E RADICCHIO

Tonnarelli with Sausage and Radicchio

Tonnarelli are thick *spaghetti* eaten in Lazio and in the region of Abruzzo, where this type of pasta is more commonly known as *spaghetti alla chittara* because the special gadget needed to make it resembles guitar strings. If you can get this gadget, then you can make the *tonnarelli*, otherwise use the spaghetti attachment on your pasta machine, but make the *spaghetti* thicker than usual. The robust sauce of sausage meat and pecorino marries well with the slightly bitter radicchio, which adds a lighter touch to this traditional Roman pasta dish.

Serves 4

1 quantity of Egg Pasta Dough
(see page 79)

For the sauce:

2 tablespoons extra-virgin olive oil

1 onion, finely chopped

7 oz (200 g) Italian pork sausage, skinned and meat crumbled

⅔ cup (150 ml) white wine

7 oz (200 g) radicchio, finely sliced

½ cup (1¾ oz/50 g) grated pecorino, plus some extra shavings to serve

sea salt and freshly ground black pepper

Make the pasta dough as described on page 79, then roll it out slightly thicker than usual, using the number 3 setting on your pasta machine as the last setting for the dough to pass through, until it is about ⅛ in (3 mm). Fix the *spaghetti*-making attachment to your machine and extrude the dough into thick *spaghetti*. If you don't have one, cut out long thick strands by hand with a sharp knife. Set aside.

Heat the olive oil in a large frying pan over medium heat, add the onion, and sweat for 1–2 minutes. Add the crumbled sausage meat and cook until well seared, then increase the heat, add the white wine, and allow to evaporate. Add the radicchio and some salt and pepper to taste, and sauté for about 7 minutes, until the radicchio is cooked but still slightly crunchy.

Meanwhile, bring a large saucepan of salted water to a boil and cook the *tonnarelli* for 1–2 minutes or until *al dente*.

Drain the pasta, add it to the sauce, along with the grated pecorino, and mix well together over high heat for 1 minute. Remove from the heat and serve with shavings of pecorino.

FARFALLE CON ZUCCHINE MISTE E SPECK

Farfalle with Mixed Zucchini and Speck

A perfect recipe for the end of summer when zucchini are plentiful and you get the yellow summer squash too! The combination of grated zucchini and zucchini matchsticks gives a pleasant contrast in texture. For vegetarians, omit the speck. Fresh *farfalle* pasta is easily obtainable in stores, but you could make your own using the Egg Pasta Dough recipe on page 79.

Serves 4

11½ oz (325 g) fresh *farfalle* pasta

14 oz (400 g) mixed zucchini and yellow summer squash

4 tablespoons extra-virgin olive oil

1 banana shallot, finely chopped

7 oz (200 g) speck, sliced into small thin strips

10 mint leaves

sea salt and freshly ground black pepper

If making your own *farfalle*, make the pasta dough as described on page 79.

Grate half of the mixed zucchini and yellow squash on the large holes of a grater. Cut the other half into thin julienne strips or matchsticks and set aside.

Heat 2 tablespoons of the olive oil in a frying pan over low heat, add the shallot, and sweat for about 10 minutes, adding a couple of tablespoons of hot water, until the shallots become soft and translucent. Add the grated zucchini with another tablespoon of hot water, season with a little salt and pepper, and cook gently for about 5 minutes until softened.

Meanwhile, heat the remaining olive oil in a separate frying pan, add the zucchini matchsticks, and sauté over medium heat for 4–5 minutes, until soft and slightly colored. Remove from the heat and set aside.

Bring a large saucepan of salted water to a boil and cook the *farfalle* for 1–2 minutes until *al dente*.

Combine the speck with the grated zucchini mixture. Drain the *farfalle* and add to the pan with the speck, mix well, and cook over medium high heat for 1 minute. Remove from the heat and serve with the zucchini matchsticks, sprinkled with mint leaves and a grinding of black pepper.

FUSILLI CON CONIGLIO E PROFUMO D'ARANCIA

Fusilli with Rabbit and Orange

This delicious rustic dish is cooked in a slightly unusual way. Instead of starting with the typical *soffritto*, the rabbit is delicately cooked in olive oil and wine before the vegetables and orange juice are added; it is then cooked over low heat until all the liquid is absorbed, giving both meat and vegetables a delicious flavor. The orange marries perfectly with the rabbit, giving it a nice kick and enhancing its delicate taste. If you can find *trottole*, little twists of pasta, use them. If you prefer, you can substitute the rabbit with chicken breast.

Serves 4

1 lb 4 oz (550 g) rabbit

¼ cup (60 ml) extra-virgin olive oil

2 rosemary sprigs

1¼ cups (300 ml) white wine

2 banana shallots, finely chopped

1 large carrot, finely chopped

1 celery stalk, finely chopped

zest and juice of 1 orange

11½ oz (325 g) fresh *fusilli* pasta (or use dried)

sea salt and freshly ground black pepper

grated pecorino, to serve

Remove and discard the bones from the rabbit and coarsely chop the meat into small chunks (you could ask your butcher to do this).

In a large saucepan, combine the rabbit, olive oil, rosemary, and white wine. Season with some salt and pepper, and cook over medium heat for 12–15 minutes, until all the liquid has been absorbed. Increase the heat and stir in the vegetables and orange juice. Reduce the heat, cover, and cook for about 6 minutes, until the orange juice has evaporated. Add about ¼ cup (60 ml) of hot water and continue to cook, covered, over low heat for 10–12 minutes, until the vegetables are tender.

Meanwhile, bring a large saucepan of salted water to a boil and cook the *fusilli* until *al dente* (check the instructions on your package for cooking time).

Drain the pasta, add it to the sauce, and mix well over high heat for about 1 minute, until well combined. Remove from the heat and serve, sprinkled with the orange zest and some freshly grated pecorino.

Fresh Pasta

FILLED PASTA

Filled pasta, like pasta itself, is ancient in origin and there are many, often conflicting, theories on how the various recipes came about. Whatever the origins, we do know that filled pasta plays an important part in Italian gastronomy, especially in the northern and central regions where it is traditionally made on Sundays or for feast days such as Christmas.

The basic concept has remained the same: wafer-thin pasta dough is cut into squares or circles, filled with meat, vegetables, fish, or cheese, then wrapped into a parcel. There are so many different shapes, different fillings and, of course, each type can be accompanied with a different sauce. As with all Italian food, these vary according to regions, towns, and villages, and even families have their own favorites.

In Bologna, *tortellini* filled with prosciutto are traditionally served in a light broth; in the towns of Parma and Piacenza, half-moon *agnolini* stuffed with pot-roasted meat are popular served in broth or with a sauce. In Piemonte, *agnolotti* filled with various meats and vegetables are traditional. Liguria has *pansotti* filled with local greens and cheese; meaty *casoncelli* are eaten in Bergamo in Lombardy; and *tortelli* with pumpkin are a speciality of Cremona. In Sardinia, *culurzones* are filled with mashed potato, cheese, and mint; and their deep-fried *seadas* have a sweet filling.

In this chapter, I have given you recipes for a few of my favorite filled pastas, but there are so, so many more. If you prefer, you can make them into different shapes, use other fillings, or even invent your own—leftover roast meat and veggies make excellent fillings. They do take a little time, patience, and love, but these delicious little parcels of joy are worth it. You can always make more and freeze them to enjoy at another time—they don't need defrosting, since you can cook them from frozen. Serve with a quick butter and sage sauce and you can be enjoying a good, nutritious homemade meal in no time.

MARUBINI AL BRODO DI TRE CARNI DELLA MAMMA DI PAOLO

Marubini in a Three-Meat Broth

This recipe comes from my friend Paolo from Cremona in northern Italy, which is where these delicious parcels of meaty goodness originate, and are enjoyed for Christmas lunch or other special occasions. The quantities are quite large— firstly, because you need a certain amount of meat to make the broth and, in turn, that cooked meat is used as the filling for the *marubini*; secondly, because their traditional place is on the table at special feasts, when it is typical to cook for a crowd. If you are not feeding this many, you can freeze them for another time. If you prefer, you can also enjoy them *all'asciuto* (without the broth) and serve them in Butter and Sage Sauce (see page 166). Don't waste the broth—you can use it as stock or for soups. I dedicate this recipe to Paolo's late mom, who made this dish for her family and passed the recipe down to her son, so I too am able to enjoy this delicious filled pasta in broth.

For the *Brodo di Tre Carni*:

Makes about 10½ cups (2.5 liters)

14 oz (400 g) skirt steak or brisket

1 pork chop, on-the-bone
  (about 9 oz/250 g)

1 chicken leg quarter (about 9 oz/250 g)

1 large onion, quartered

2 celery stalks with leaves, halved

2 carrots, scrubbed and left whole

a handful of parsley

10½ cups (2.5 liters) stock—use chicken or
  beef, or a mixture of both

To make the *Brodo di Tre Carni*: place all the ingredients into a very large heavy stockpot and bring to a boil. Skim the fat from the surface, cover with a lid, lower the heat, and leave to simmer gently for about 2 hours, until all the meats are well cooked.

Remove the meats and set aside for making the *marubini* filling (overleaf). Pass the broth through a fine sieve.

Use for cooking *marubini*, continuing with the recipe as decribed overleaf; or use for *Pastina* Soup (see page 27). If not using immediately, allow to cool completely, then transfer to an airtight container. The broth will keep for up to 3 days in the refrigerator or for up to 3 months if frozen.

Filled Pasta

Filled Pasta 113

Filled Pasta

For the *Marubini*:

Serves 10–12 (makes about 120)

1 quantity of *Brodo di Tre Carni*
  (see page 112)

2 x quantities of Egg Pasta Dough
  (see page 79)

Italian "00" pasta flour, for dusting

1 egg, beaten

fine semolina, for sprinkling

For the filling:

cooked beef, pork, and chicken from
  Brodo di Tre Carni (see page 112)

1 tablespoon extra virgin olive oil

pat of butter

1 banana shallot, finely chopped

2 bay leaves

leaves of 2 thyme sprigs

scant ½ cup (100 ml) white wine

1½ oz (40 g) salami

1½ oz (40 g) mortadella (cured pork sausage)

1 egg

½ cup (1¾ oz/50 g) grated Parmesan,
  plus extra to serve

sea salt and freshly ground black pepper

To make the *Marubini*: make the broth as described on page 112 and the pasta dough as described on page 79.

To make the filling, allow the cooked meat from making the broth to cool slightly, until you can handle it easily, then pull the meat from the bones. Discard the bones, along with any chicken skin. Roughly chop the meats and set aside.

Heat the olive oil and butter in a frying pan set over medium heat, add the shallot and bay leaves, and sweat for 2 minutes, or until the shallot has softened. Add the chopped meats and thyme leaves, increase the heat to high, and fry, stirring, for 2 minutes. Add the white wine, allow to evaporate, then reduce the heat to medium and continue to cook for a further 3 minutes. Remove from the heat and let cool.

When cool, transfer the mixture to a food processor, add the salami and mortadella, and process until everything is finely chopped. Add the egg, grated Parmesan, and some salt and pepper, and continue to process until you obtain a smooth consistency. Set aside.

Since pasta dough dries out quickly, it's best to do this next step in batches—taking just a little pasta dough out of the refrigerator at a time.

Roll out a small amount of the pasta dough on a lightly floured work surface until wafer-thin (or to the thinnest setting on a pasta machine—about ¹⁄₁₆ in/2 mm). Cut the dough into 2 in (5 cm) diameter circles and brush each with egg wash. Place small balls of filling in the middle of each circle, then fold the circles over the filling into half-moon shapes. Press to seal. Place the filled *marubini* on a tray sprinkled with some fine semolina.

Bring the broth back to a boil in a large saucepan, add the *marubini*, and cook for 5–6 minutes. Remove from the heat and serve in individual soup bowls with a sprinkling of freshly grated Parmesan.

CASONCELLI CON CARNE MACINATA

Casoncelli with Mixed Meats

This typical filled pasta comes from the northern region of Lombardy. As with many Italian recipes, this dish originated in the housewife's kitchen as a way of using up meat leftovers. There are many versions throughout the region, and some towns and villages enjoy a sweeter version, including crunchy *amaretti* biscuits and raisins in the filling. I like this simple version with a mix of ground beef and pork, mortadella (cured pork sausage), and grated Parmesan. You can of course use other meats, such as Italian sausage meat, salami, or leftover meat from a roast. Served with a rich butter and sage sauce and lots of grated Parmesan, this dish is a Sunday lunch favorite in many northern Italian households.

Serves 4–6 (makes about 35 *casoncelli*)

1 quantity of Egg Pasta Dough
  (see page 79)

Italian "00" pasta flour, for dusting

1 egg, beaten

1 quantity of Butter and Sage Sauce
  (see page 166)

sea salt

grated Parmesan, to serve

For the filling:

1 tablespoon extra-virgin olive oil

1 small onion, finely chopped

3½ oz (100 g) ground beef

3½ oz (100 g) ground pork

leaves of 1 rosemary sprig, finely chopped

3½ oz (100 g) mortadella (cured pork
  sausage), finely chopped

1 cup (3½ oz/100 g) grated Parmesan

scant 1 cup (1¾ oz/50 g) dried breadcrumbs

1 egg, beaten

sea salt and freshly ground black pepper

Make the pasta dough as described on page 79.

To make the filling, heat the olive oil in a frying pan over high heat, add the onion, and sweat for 2 minutes until softened. Add the ground meats and rosemary, and fry, stirring, until the meat is well seared. Lower the heat and cook for about 15 minutes.

Remove from the heat, let cool slightly, then add the mortadella, grated Parmesan, breadcrumbs, egg, and some salt and pepper. Mix well to combine (it might be easier to do this with your hands).

On a lightly floured work surface, roll out the pasta dough until wafer-thin (or to the thinnest setting on a pasta machine). Cut into 2¾ in (7 cm) squares, and brush with egg wash. Place a small ball of filling into the middle of each square, then fold the dough over the filling to form a triangle, pressing well along the edges to seal. Take the two points at the base of each triangle and bring together, pinching firmly to join.

Bring a large saucepan of salted water to a boil, add the *casoncelli,* and cook for about 8 minutes. Drain and serve with Butter and Sage Sauce and a good sprinkling of freshly grated Parmesan.

RAVIOLI AL PESCE SERVITI CON SALSA DI POMODORINI FRESCHI

Seabream Ravioli with Capers and Lemon Zest in Cherry Tomato Sauce

In this dish, delicate seabream combines really well with a punchy tomato sauce, bringing out the taste of the Mediterranean. You could also use another white fish such as hake, cod, or seabass (make sure it is filleted and free of bones). This is a perfect dish for summer months, served with a glass of cold, crisp *Greco di Tufo*.

Serves 4–6 (makes about 24 round ravioli)

1 quantity of Eggless Pasta Dough (see page 79)

Italian "00" pasta flour, for dusting

1 egg, beaten

sea salt

For the filling:

1 tablespoon extra-virgin olive oil

1 garlic clove, left whole

2 anchovy fillets

7 oz (200 g) sea bream fillets

1 teaspoon capers

1 tablespoon finely chopped parsley

1 teaspoon lemon zest

For the sauce:

3 tablespoons extra-virgin olive oil

2 garlic cloves, left whole

3 anchovy fillets

2 teaspoons capers

⅓ cup (1½ oz/40 g) green or black olives, coarsely chopped

14 oz (400 g) cherry tomatoes, quartered

a handful of parsley, finely chopped

Make the eggless pasta dough as described on page 79.

To make the filling, heat the olive oil in a saucepan over medium heat, add the garlic and anchovy fillets, and sweat until the anchovies have melted. Add the seabream, capers, and 1 tablespoon water, cover with a lid, and cook for about 5 minutes, until the fish has cooked through. Remove from the heat, discard the garlic, and leave to cool slightly. Transfer the mixture to a chopping board. Flake the fish and finely chop the capers (alternatively, transfer the mixture to a food processor and pulse until well combined), then mix with the parsley and lemon zest.

On a lightly floured work surface, roll out the pasta dough until wafer-thin (or to the thinnest setting on a pasta machine). Use a 2½ in (6.5 cm) diameter round pastry cutter to cut out circles, then brush each one with egg wash. Place a little filling in the center of half of the circles, then place the remaining circles on top to cover, pressing firmly around the edges with your fingers so that the filling does not escape.

To make the sauce, heat the olive oil in a saucepan over medium heat, add the garlic and anchovy fillets, and sweat until the anchovies have melted. Discard the garlic clove, add the capers and olives, and sweat for 1 minute. Add the cherry tomatoes and a little of the parsley, cover with a lid, and cook over a medium–high heat for 2 minutes. Reduce the heat to low and cook for a further 5 minutes.

Meanwhile, bring a large saucepan of salted water to a boil, add the ravioli, and cook for about 7 minutes. Drain and serve with the sauce, sprinkled with the remaining parsley.

CARAMELLE CON VERDURE DI PRIMAVERA

Caramelle with Spring Vegetables

What better way to celebrate the arrival of spring, with its sweet, succulent vegetables, than with this delicious filled pasta recipe? Get the kids to help wrap up the *caramelle* (which translates as "candies")—they are packed full of green goodness!

Serves 4–6 (makes about 30 *caramelle*)

1 quantity of Egg Pasta Dough
  (see page 79)

1 quantity of Basic Tomato Sauce
  (see page 162)

Italian "00" pasta flour, for dusting

1 egg, beaten

sea salt

Parmesan shavings and fresh basil leaves,
  to serve

For the filling:

¾ cup (3½ oz/100 g) fresh or frozen peas

1 tablespoon extra-virgin olive oil

1 small banana shallot, finely chopped

2 oz (60 g) asparagus tips, finely chopped

3 oz (85 g) zucchini, finely chopped

12 basil leaves, finely chopped

¼ cup (2 oz/60 g) ricotta

2 tablespoons grated Parmesan

Make the pasta dough as described on page 79 and the tomato sauce as on page 162.

For the filling, cook the fresh peas in boiling water for 4 minutes, drain, and set aside. Skip this step if you are using frozen peas.

Heat the olive oil in a saucepan over medium heat, add the shallot, and sweat for 2 minutes. Add the peas, asparagus, zucchini, and a couple of chopped basil leaves, and fry, stirring, for a minute or so. Add 2 tablespoons of water and cook for about 10 minutes, until the vegetables are tender. Remove from the heat, let cool slightly, then add the remaining basil and the ricotta and Parmesan, and mix well to combine.

On a lightly floured work surface, roll out the pasta dough until wafer-thin (or to the thinnest setting on a pasta machine). Cut into rectangles about 2¾ x 1½ in (7 x 4 cm) and brush with egg wash. Place some filling in the middle of each, along the longer side of the rectangles, and roll up to resemble a candy wrapper, pinching both sides well so that the filling does not escape.

Cook the *caramelle* in plenty of salted boiling water for about 9 minutes, then drain and mix with the tomato sauce. Serve immediately with Parmesan shavings and basil leaves.

PIATTO UNICO DI CAPO D'ANNO

Cotechino Cappellacci on a Bed of Lentils

Cotechino, the rich pork sausage traditionally served with lentils on New Year's Eve in Italy, makes the perfect filling for delicious *cappellacci* pasta. As the name suggests, *cappellacci* are shaped like little hats. My recipe title translates as "New Year's Main Course" because it combines all the foods eaten on this day—even the pasta course. Rich, substantial, and delicious, it is the perfect dish for that time of year.

Serves 4–6 (makes about 48 *cappellacci*)

1 quantity of Egg Pasta Dough (see page 79)

Italian "00" pasta flour, for dusting

1 egg, beaten

2 tablespoons extra-virgin olive oil, plus extra to serve

1 rosemary sprig

2 sage leaves

sea salt

grated Parmesan, to serve

For the filling:

9 oz (250 g) pre-cooked vacuum-packed *cotechino* sausage

1 potato, peeled and cut into chunks

5 tablespoons ricotta

3 tablespoons grated Parmesan

For the lentils:

1 cup (7 oz/200 g) small green or brown lentils

1 bay leaf

1 garlic clove, left whole

1 small carrot, chopped

1 banana shallot, finely chopped

1 tablespoon extra-virgin olive oil

4¼ cups (1 liter) vegetable stock

sea salt and freshly ground black pepper

Make the pasta dough as described on page 79. Wrap it in plastic wrap and refrigerate while you make the filling and lentils.

For the filling, put the pack of *cotechino* into a saucepan, cover with cold water, bring to a boil, and simmer for 20 minutes (or according to the package directions). Drain, then carefully cut open the package and drain off any excess liquid. Transfer to a large bowl.

Meanwhile, cook the potato in boiling water until tender. Drain and combine it with the *cotechino*, then add the ricotta and Parmesan, and mash with a fork until well combined and fairly smooth. Set aside.

Put all the ingredients for the lentils in a large pot, bring to a boil, then gently simmer for 20–30 minutes, until the lentils are tender (check the package directions). Add salt and pepper if necessary. Discard the garlic and bay leaf, set aside, and keep warm.

On a floured surface, roll out the pasta dough to ¼ in (5 mm) thick and cut into 2½ in (6.5 cm) squares. Brush each square with beaten egg, place a heaped teaspoon of the *cotechino* mixture in the middle, then fold the pasta over into a triangle shape, enclosing the filling. Press down the edges to seal. Take the two corners on the long edge of the triangles and fold them to join each other at the bottom of the triangles. Press firmly to secure. You should have made little hat shapes.

Bring a large saucepan of salted water to a boil, add the *cappellacci,* and cook for 3–4 minutes.

Meanwhile, in a large frying pan, heat the olive oil with the rosemary and sage over medium heat and add the cooked lentils. Transfer the cooked *cappellacci* to the pan with a slotted spoon and cook for 1 minute or so. Serve immediately, with Parmesan and olive oil.

PANSOTTI LIGURI CON SALSA ALLE NOCI

Ligurian Swiss Chard Pansotti in a Walnut Sauce

These eggless pasta parcels are a speciality of Liguria, where the filling is usually made with local greens known as *preboggion*, which grow wild along the coast. When these greens are not available, Swiss chard, spinach, or borage can also be used. The origins of this recipe are uncertain, however it is said they were probably made during Lent, when meat was forbidden. The word *pansotti* means "belly" in the Ligurian dialect: the parcels are filled quite generously and resemble large bellies. Paired with a delicious walnut sauce that adds a nice crunch, these *pansotti* are very welcome in my belly!

Serves 4 (makes about 24 *pansotti*)

1 quantity of Eggless Pasta Dough
  (see page 79)

Italian "00" pasta flour, for dusting

1 egg, beaten

sea salt

For the filling:

14 oz (400 g) Swiss chard or rainbow chard

2 tablespoons extra-virgin olive oil

2 garlic cloves, left whole

scant ½ cup (3½ oz/100 g) ricotta

scant ½ cup (1½ oz/40 g) grated Parmesan

a few thyme leaves

1 egg, beaten

sea salt and freshly ground black pepper

For the walnut sauce:

¾ oz (20 g) bread

⅓ cup (80 ml) milk

⅔ cup (3 oz/85 g) walnut halves

1 garlic clove

a few thyme leaves, plus extra to serve

3 tablespoons pine nuts

3 tablespoons grated Parmesan

Make the eggless pasta dough as described on page 79.

To make the filling, wash the chard, then remove the stalks (keep them for another recipe). Roughly chop the leaves and set aside.

In a large frying pan, heat the olive oil over medium heat, add the garlic, and sweat for 1 minute. Add the chard and some salt, lower the heat, cover the pan, and cook for about 5 minutes until softened. Remove from the heat, discard the garlic, then drain and squeeze out any excess liquid from the chard—you may have to squeeze it between your hands to do this well. In a large bowl, combine the chard with the ricotta, grated Parmesan, thyme leaves, beaten egg, and some black pepper.

On a lightly floured work surface, roll out the pasta dough until wafer-thin (or to the thinnest setting on a pasta machine). Cut the dough into 2¾ in (7 cm) squares and brush each with egg wash. Place a little filling in the middle of each, then fold the dough over the filling to form a triangle. Press to seal.

Bring a large saucepan of salted water to a boil, add the *pansotti,* and cook for about 4 minutes.

To make the sauce, soak the bread in the milk for about a minute, to soften, then place all the ingredients in a food processor and process until smooth. Transfer to a large frying pan and heat through.

Using a slotted spoon, transfer the *pansotti* to the walnut sauce, with perhaps a little of the hot pasta cooking water, mixing well to combine. Heat through and serve immediately, sprinkled with thyme.

Filled Pasta

CULURZONES

Sardinian Culurzones with Potato, Pecorino, and Mint

This traditional filled pasta from Sardinia, also known as *culurgiones* or *culinjonis*, can have various fillings—however, the shape, which represents a wheat sheaf, always remains the same. It's quite a tricky shape to master at first, but with a little practice you will get the hang of it. They were traditionally made to celebrate the wheat harvest, and this is probably how the shape evolved. It is said that they were also made to ward off death and eaten on the Day of the Dead, on November 2. I like to eat them at any time—they are so delicious that, once you start, you can't stop!

Serves 4 (makes about 36 *culurzones*)

1 quantity of Egg Pasta Dough
(see page 79)

1 quantity of Basic Tomato Sauce
(see page 162)

Italian "00" pasta flour, for dusting

a handful of basil leaves, to serve

sea salt

For the filling:

1 lb 2 oz (500 g) potatoes, peeled and cut into chunks

splash of extra-virgin olive oil

1 onion, very finely chopped

¾ cup (2½ oz/70 g) grated pecorino, plus extra to serve

10 mint leaves, very finely chopped

sea salt and freshly ground black pepper

Make the eggless pasta dough as described on page 79 and the tomato sauce as described on page 162.

To make the filling, cook the potatoes in boiling water until tender.

Meanwhile, heat the olive oil in a small frying pan over medium–low heat, add the onion, and sweat, covered with a lid, for about 10 minutes until softened.

Drain the cooked potatoes and let steam-dry for a couple of minutes, to make sure all the moisture evaporates. Mash the potatoes (I like to use a ricer), then thoroughly combine with the softened onions, grated pecorino, and chopped mint, adding salt and pepper to taste. Set aside.

On a lightly floured work surface, roll out the pasta dough until wafer-thin (or to the thinnest setting on a pasta machine). Cut the dough into 4 in (10 cm) circles. Place a good amount of the filling (roughly the size of a walnut) in the middle of each pasta circle and brush the edges with a little water. Take each circle in your hand, gently close in half, then pinch a fold of the dough over from the right, and then the left, side to create a pleated effect. Pinch the top to seal.

Bring a large saucepan of salted water to a boil, add the *culurzones*, and cook for 3–4 minutes.

Meanwhile, heat the tomato sauce in a large frying pan. Using a slotted spoon or pasta spider, transfer the *culurzones* to the tomato sauce, just gently coating them to ensure you don't break them. Serve immediately with a sprinkling of grated pecorino and some basil.

TORTELLONI CON FUNGHI E NOCI CON SALSA AL GUANCIALE

Mushroom and Walnut Tortelloni with Guanciale Sauce

A delicious combination of cultivated cremini mushrooms and crunchy walnuts fill these *tortelloni*, a larger version of the popular *tortellini*. Served with a tasty sauce of *guanciale* and tomato, it makes a delicious autumnal meal. *Guanciale* is cured pork cheek, which really adds flavor to the sauce. It is obtainable from good Italian delis, but you could substitute with some good smoky pancetta.

Serves 4 (makes about 24 *tortelloni*)
1 quantity of Egg Pasta Dough (see page 79)
Italian "00" pasta flour, for dusting
1 egg, beaten
grated Parmesan, to serve
sea salt

For the filling:
2 tablespoons extra-virgin olive oil
1 small banana shallot, finely chopped
12 oz (350 g) cremini mushrooms, very finely chopped
scant ½ cup (1¾ oz/50 g) walnuts, very finely chopped
1 potato, peeled, boiled, and mashed
scant ½ cup (1½ oz/40 g) grated Parmesan
sea salt and freshly ground black pepper

For the sauce:
2 tablespoons extra-virgin olive oil
5½ oz (150 g) *guanciale* (cured pork cheek), finely diced
1 small onion, finely chopped
1 x 14 oz (400 g) can of chopped tomatoes
sea salt and freshly ground black pepper

Make the pasta dough as described on page 79.

To make the filling, heat the olive oil in a frying pan over medium heat, add the shallot and sweat for 2 minutes. Increase the heat, add the mushrooms and fry, stirring, for 2 minutes. Reduce the heat to medium, add some salt and pepper, and cook for about 10 minutes, until the mushrooms are cooked through. If necessary, drain off any excess liquid, then stir in the walnuts and mashed potato and cook for a further minute or so. Remove from the heat, stir in the grated Parmesan and check the seasoning. Set aside.

To make the sauce, heat the olive oil in a saucepan over medium–high heat, add the *guanciale,* and fry, stirring, for 2 minutes, until golden. Reduce the heat, add the onion, and sweat for 2 minutes. Stir in the tomatoes, cover the pan, and cook over medium heat for 25 minutes. Season with salt and pepper to taste and keep warm.

Meanwhile, on a floured work surface, roll out the pasta dough until wafer-thin (or to the thinnest setting on a pasta machine). Cut the dough into 3 in (8 cm) squares, and brush each with egg wash. Place a teaspoonful of filling in the middle of each and fold over into a triangle shape, pressing the edges firmly together. Bring the two corners of the long edge around to meet each other in a circle, and press together to seal.

Bring a large saucepan of salted water to a boil, add the *tortelloni,* and cook for 3 minutes. Drain with a slotted spoon and serve with the *guanciale* sauce and a sprinkling of grated Parmesan.

Filled Pasta

BAULETTI DI BROCCOLI E SALSICCIA

Broccoli and Sausage Parcels in Tomato Sauce

Sausages with broccoli is a very popular dish in the Campania region of southern Italy and one of my favorite meals when I'm there! I've combined these simple ingredients to fill these pasta parcels, made with an eggless dough that is common in the south. *Bauletti* translates as "little treasure chests." Served with a light tomato sauce, these pasta parcels make a delicious and wholesome meal for the whole family to enjoy.

Serves 4 (makes about 24 *bauletti*)

1 quantity of Eggless Pasta Dough
   (see page 79)
Italian "00" pasta flour, for dusting
1 egg, beaten
sea salt

For the filling:

5½ oz (150 g) broccoli florets
2 tablespoons extra-virgin olive oil
2 garlic cloves
½ red chili pepper
5½ oz (150 g) Italian pork sausages, skinned
   and crumbled

For the sauce:

1 x 14 oz (400 g) can of plum tomatoes,
   drained (save the juice to use in
   another recipe)
2 tablespoons extra-virgin olive oil
2 garlic cloves, thinly sliced
sea salt

Make the eggless pasta dough as described on page 79.

To make the filling, cook the broccoli florets in boiling water for about 5 minutes, until just tender but not mushy, then drain and set aside.

Meanwhile, heat the olive oil in a frying pan over medium heat, add the garlic and chili, and sweat for 1 minute. Add the sausage meat and fry, stirring, for 2 minutes, or until the sausage meat is seared.

Drain the broccoli florets, retaining about 1 tablespoon of the cooking water, and add them to the pan with the sausage meat. Cover the pan and cook over medium heat for about 7 minutes. Remove from the heat, discard the garlic, let cool a little, then mix until well combined. Set aside.

On a lightly floured work surface, roll out the pasta dough until wafer-thin (or to the thinnest setting on a pasta machine). Cut the dough into 3 in (8 cm) squares and brush all over with egg wash. Place some filling in the middle of each square, then fold in each of the corners to the center to form little square parcels, firmly pinching along the joins to seal.

To make the sauce, slice the plum tomatoes lengthways. Heat the olive oil in a small saucepan over medium heat, add the garlic, and sweat for a minute or so. Add the sliced tomatoes, season with some salt, and cook gently for 3–4 minutes.

Cook the *bauletti* parcels in plenty of salted boiling water for 6–7 minutes, then drain and serve with the tomato sauce.

MEZZELUNE CON ZUCCA E TALEGGIO

Mezzelune with Butternut Squash and Taleggio

This is my version of *tortelli di zucca*, so popular in northern Italy during the fall, when pumpkins are in abundance. In place of the more typical ricotta, I have used taleggio, the strong-flavored soft cheese of Lombardy, which gives a kick to the butternut squash. The addition of almonds gives the dish a nice crunch.

Serves 4–6 (makes about 60 *mezzelune*)

1 quantity of Egg Pasta Dough
   (see page 79)

Italian "00" pasta flour, for dusting

1 egg, beaten

1 quantity of Butter and Sage Sauce
   (see page 166)

sea salt

1 tablespoon slivered almonds, lightly toasted,
   to serve

For the filling:

1 tablespoon extra-virgin olive oil

2 oz (60 g) pancetta, finely chopped

1 small banana shallot, finely chopped

needles of 1 rosemary sprig, finely chopped

1¾ cups (9 oz/250 g) small butternut
   squash cubes

1¾ oz (50 g) taleggio cheese, cut into cubes

1 tablespoon breadcrumbs, plus more
   if needed

1 tablespoon slivered almonds,
   finely chopped

sea salt and freshly ground black pepper

Make the pasta dough as described on page 79.

To make the filling, heat the olive oil in a frying pan over medium heat, add the pancetta, and fry, stirring, for 2 minutes. Add the shallot and rosemary, and sweat for 3 minutes. Stir in the butternut squash, add 2 tablespoons water, cover the pan, and cook for 12–15 minutes, until the butternut squash has softened. Remove from the heat and, using a potato masher or fork, mash the butternut squash mixture until smooth. Stir in the taleggio, breadcrumbs, chopped almonds, and some salt and pepper. If the mixture appears too wet, add some more breadcrumbs.

On a lightly floured work surface, roll out the pasta dough until wafer-thin (or to the thinnest setting on a pasta machine). Cut the dough into 2½ in (6 cm) circles and brush each with egg wash. Place small dollops of the filling in the middle of each circle, then fold the dough over the filling into half-moon shapes. Press to seal.

Bring a large saucepan of salted water to a boil, add the *mezzelune,* and cook for about 5 minutes.

Make the butter and sage sauce as described on page 166.

Remove the *mezzelune* with a slotted spoon and gently stir into the butter and sage sauce. Serve immediately, sprinkled with toasted almonds.

BAKED PASTA

I love baked pasta dishes. When I was a child, we would have pasta *al forno* for special occasions, which would be lovingly baked in our grandfather's wood-fired oven. For southern Italians, a baked pasta dish is as special as filled pasta is in the north of Italy, since some recipes can take a lot of time to prepare. At Christmas, we would enjoy a festive *lasagne*, with fresh pasta sheets made by my mother, a ragù sauce made by my zia Maria, and meatballs patiently rolled by my sisters. It was such a huge and nutritious dish that a small square of it would suffice, but also because this was just our appetizer course!

Baked pasta is a great way of using up leftovers and this is probably how it originated. Leftover cheese, cured meats, and tomato sauce are perfect ingredients—mix these with some cooked pasta, pour into an ovenproof dish, sprinkle with lots of Parmesan or pecorino, bake in a hot oven, and you get a wonderful, nutritious dish with minimum effort.

Again, as with all pasta dishes, there are regional variations. The traditional *lasagne* with a Bolognese ragù and white sauce, known locally as *Lasagne Emiliane*, originates from the Bologna region and its popularity has spread worldwide. Of course, there are many more varieties all over Italy, and you can enjoy lighter versions with vegetables and ricotta cheese or with seafood. *Cannelloni* is another classic, with fillings of ground meat or spinach and ricotta.

Other popular baked shapes are *rigatoni*, *conchiglioni* (large shells), and *paccheri* (large tubes), as well as *fusilli*, which are excellent with cheese sauces.

The recipes in this chapter all use dried pasta, including *lasagne* sheets and *cannelloni*, which do not require pre-cooking, and you can find both egg and eggless varieties. You can make your own fresh pasta sheets (see page 79), however these will need to be blanched and dried with paper towels before baking. I always keep packages of dried *lasagne* sheets and *cannelloni* tubes in my pantry, since these baked pasta dishes are family favorites—not only made for special occasions, but often for midweek meals.

LASAGNE DI CARNEVALE

Carnival-Time Lasagne

This typical southern Italian *lasagne* is usually made for special occasions such as *Carnevale*—the week before Lent when festivities take place all over Italy. Lent is traditionally a time when eating meat is forbidden, so a *lasagne* such as this one—with meat ragù and sausage—would be made to enjoy before the period of abstinence. Only the tomato sauce from the meat ragù is used for the *lasagne*; the beef can then be enjoyed as a second course with a green salad.

Serves 6

9 oz (250 g) Italian pork sausage

splash of extra-vigin olive oil

1½ cups (12 oz/350 g) ricotta

2 eggs

1½ cups (5½ oz/150 g) grated Parmesan

sea salt and freshly ground black pepper

12 dried *lasagne* sheets

9 oz (250 g) mozzarella, coarsely chopped

For the ragù:

3 tablespoons extra-virgin olive oil

1 onion, finely chopped

2 bay leaves

1 lb 10 oz (750 g) beef brisket, cut into large chunks

⅓ cup (80 ml) red wine

1 tablespoon tomato paste dissolved in a little warm water

3 x 14 oz (400 g) cans of chopped plum tomatoes

a handful of basil leaves

3 tablespoons grated Parmesan

sea salt and freshly ground black pepper

First make the ragù: heat the olive oil in a large saucepan over medium heat, add the onion and bay leaves, and sweat for about 3 minutes, until softened. Add the beef and sear well all over. Increase the heat, add the wine, and allow to evaporate. Stir in the tomato paste mixture, chopped tomatoes, basil, Parmesan, and some salt and pepper. Bring to a boil, then reduce the heat, cover, and simmer gently for at least 2 hours, until the meat is cooked through and the sauce is thick. Check from time to time, stirring with a wooden spoon and, if necessary, add a little hot water.

When cooked, remove the beef and set aside to enjoy later.

Meanwhile, preheat the oven to 400°F (200°C).

Cook the pork sausage: you can either do this in the oven or fry it. If using the oven, put the sausage into a roasting pan with a splash of olive oil and bake for 25 minutes. If frying, fry with a splash of olive oil over medium heat for about 15 minutes. When cooked through, remove, slice, and set aside.

In a large bowl, combine the ricotta, eggs, half of the Parmesan, and some salt and pepper, until creamy.

Line the bottom of a baking dish (about 9½ x 7 in/24 x 17 cm) with some of the tomato ragù, cover with a layer of *lasagne* sheets, then add a layer of ricotta, scatter over some sausage slices and some pieces of mozzarella, then add another layer of tomato ragù. Continue making layers in this way until you have used up all the ingredients, ending with a layer of *lasagne* sheets, tomato ragù, mozzarella, and the remaining grated Parmesan sprinkled on top.

Cover with foil and bake in the hot oven for 20 minutes. Remove the foil and bake for a further 20 minutes, until golden and bubbling.

Baked Pasta

LASAGNE AI FRUTTI DI MARE

Seafood Lasagne

If you enjoy seafood, you will love this *lasagne*! It takes a little time and organization to prepare the fresh seafood and the various different elements, but once all the basics are ready, it's really simple and well worth the effort. If you can't get fresh seafood or don't have the time, use a 2 lb 4 oz (1 kg) bag of prepared mixed seafood instead, which you can simply sauté in a little extra-virgin olive oil with a little chopped garlic and parsley, then proceed to assemble the *lasagne* as directed.

Serves 8

10–12 dried eggless *lasagne* sheets

For the seafood mix:

10½ oz (300 g) octopus (ask your fishmonger to clean)

10½ oz (300 g) calamari (ask your fishmonger to clean)

1 lb 2 oz (500 g) fresh mussels, washed, de-bearded, and any open shells discarded

1 lb 2 oz (500 g) fresh clams, washed and any open shells discarded

a splash of white wine

3 garlic cloves: 1 left whole, 2 finely chopped

3 tablespoons extra-virgin olive oil

7 oz (200 g) peeled shrimp

2 tablespoons finely chopped parsley, plus extra leaves to serve

For the sautéed tomatoes:

2 tablespoons extra-virgin olive oil

1 garlic clove, finely chopped

9 oz (250 g) cherry tomatoes, halved

1 tablespoon finely chopped parsley

sea salt

For the white sauce:

3 cups (700 ml) hot fish stock

3½ tablespoons (1¾ oz/50 g) butter

scant ½ cup (1¾ oz/50 g) all-purpose flour

For the gratin mixture:

¾ cup (1½ oz/40 g) fresh breadcrumbs

1 tablespoon finely chopped parsley

Bring a large saucepan of water to a boil and cook the octopus for 30–40 minutes, until tender. Remove from the heat and leave to cool in the water until you are ready to use, then roughly chop into small chunks.

In another saucepan, cook the calamari in boiling water for about 20 minutes, until tender. Leave to cool, then chop into small chunks.

Put the cleaned mussels and clams into a large saucepan with a splash of white wine and the whole garlic clove, cover with a tightly fitting lid, and cook over medium heat for 3–5 minutes, until the shells have opened. Discard any shells that have not opened. Remove from the heat and, when cool enough to handle, remove the flesh from the shells, reserving a few in their shells to garnish, if you like. Pass the cooking liquid through a fine sieve, and set aside.

Preheat the oven to 400°F (200°C).

Meanwhile, prepare the other elements.

To make the sautéed tomatoes, heat the olive oil in a pan over medium heat, add the garlic, and sweat for 1 minute. Add the cherry tomatoes, parsley, and a little salt to taste, and sauté over medium–high heat for about 3 minutes, until tender but not mushy (the tomatoes must still retain their shape). Remove from the heat and set aside.

To make the white sauce, combine the hot fish stock with the liquid left from cooking the mussels and clams. Melt the butter in a saucepan, then remove from the heat and whisk in the flour. Add a little of the stock and mix to a smooth paste. Return the pan to medium heat, gradually whisk in all of the remaining stock, and cook until the sauce begins to thicken. Remove from the heat and set aside.

For the gratin mixture, combine the breadcrumbs and parsley, and set aside.

To finish cooking the seafood, heat the olive oil in a large frying pan over medium heat, add the chopped garlic, and sweat for 1 minute. Add the mussels, clams, octopus, calamari, shrimp, and parsley, and sauté over high heat for 3 minutes. Remove and set aside.

To assemble the *lasagne*, line the bottom of a baking dish (about 9½ x 7 in/24 x 17 cm) with a little of the white sauce and top with a few sautéed tomatoes. Place a couple of *lasagne* sheets on top, followed by a layer of the seafood mixture, and a few more sautéed tomatoes. Sprinkle over some gratin mixture and then add another layer of white sauce. Continue making layers in this way until you have used up all the ingredients, ending with a layer of white sauce and a sprinkling of the gratin mixture.

Cover with foil and bake in the hot oven for 25 minutes. Remove the foil and continue to bake for 15 minutes, until just golden. Remove from the oven, leave to rest for 5 minutes and serve, garnished with the reserved shellfish and some parsley leaves.

LASAGNE CON ZUCCA

Butternut Squash Lasagne

This delicious *lasagne* is comfort food at its best, made during the fall, when butternut squash is in abundance. Simple and quick to make, it is a perfect vegetarian alternative to the traditional Bolognese *lasagne*. If you prefer, you can substitute the *dolcelatte* with fontina cheese, or even a mature cheddar.

Serves 4–6

3 tablespoons extra-virgin olive oil

1 celery stalk (with leaves), finely sliced

1 large leek (about 6 oz/175 g), finely sliced

1 garlic clove, finely chopped

needles of 2 rosemary sprigs, finely chopped

1 lb 4 oz (570 g) butternut squash, peeled and cut into small cubes

scant 1 cup (200 ml) hot vegetable stock

10–12 dried *lasagne* sheets

1¾ oz (50 g) *dolcelatte* (or Gorgonzola), coarsely chopped

2 tablespoons grated Parmesan

sea salt and freshly ground black pepper

For the white sauce:

3 tablespoons (1½ oz/40 g) butter

⅓ cup (1½ oz/40 g) all-purpose flour

generous 2 cups (500 ml) milk

scant ½ cup (1½ oz/40 g) grated Parmesan

sea salt and freshly ground black pepper

Heat the olive oil in a large saucepan over medium heat, add the celery and leek, and sweat for 2 minutes. Add the garlic and rosemary, and continue to sweat for 1 minute. Stir in the butternut squash and some salt and pepper, and continue to cook for a minute or so. Pour in the hot stock, cover with a lid, and simmer over low heat for 30 minutes.

Preheat the oven to 400°F (200°C).

Meanwhile, make the white sauce. Melt the butter in a small saucepan over medium heat. Remove from the heat and, using a small whisk, mix in the flour very quickly to avoid lumps, then gradually add the milk, whisking well. Return to the heat and cook for 3–4 minutes, whisking all the time, until the sauce begins to thicken. Remove from the heat, season with salt and pepper to taste, and stir in the grated Parmesan.

Line the bottom of a baking dish (about 9½ x 7 in/24 x 17 cm) with a little of the white sauce. Place 2–3 *lasagne* sheets on top, followed by a layer of the butternut mixture. Next, pour in another layer of the white sauce, and dot all over with pieces of *dolcelatte* cheese. Continue making layers in this way, until you have used up all the ingredients, ending with a layer of white sauce. Sprinkle with the grated Parmesan, cover with foil, and bake in the hot oven for 20 minutes.

Remove the foil and continue to bake for a further 20 minutes, until golden-brown. Remove from the oven, leave to rest for 5 minutes, then serve.

LASAGNE CON VERDURE

Vegetarian Lasagne

This light lasagne is my sister Adriana's recipe—she often makes it when catering for vegetarians. You could, if you prefer, make a white sauce (see page 167) in place of the ricotta, but using ricotta makes the dish so much lighter and is often the preferred choice in lasagne dishes throughout southern Italy.

Serves 4

6 tablespoons extra-virgin olive oil

1 red bell pepper, sliced into thin strips

1 zucchini, sliced into thin rounds

1 small eggplant, sliced into thin strips

1 cup (9 oz/250 g) ricotta

1 tablespoon milk

⅓ cup (1 oz/30 g) grated Parmesan

8–10 dried *lasagne* sheets

a handful of basil leaves

7 oz (200 g) mozzarella, cut into small cubes

sea salt and freshly ground black pepper

For the tomato sauce:

1 small banana shallot, finely chopped

1 x 14 oz (400 g) can chopped plum tomatoes

a handful of basil leaves

sea salt

Preheat the oven to 400°F (200°C).

Heat the olive oil in a saucepan and fry the peppers over medium heat for 7–10 minutes, until soft but not mushy. Using tongs, carefully transfer the peppers to a plate lined with paper towels and set aside. Fry the zucchini in the same pan for about 3 minutes on each side until cooked through, then remove and set aside. In the same pan, fry the eggplant for 5–7 minutes until cooked, then remove and set aside.

Make the tomato sauce in the same pan. Sweat the shallot in the remaining olive oil (if necessary, add an extra splash) for 2 minutes. Add the tomatoes, basil, and some salt to taste, and cook, covered, over medium heat, for about 20 minutes, stirring occasionally.

Meanwhile, in a small bowl, combine the ricotta, milk, Parmesan, and a little salt and pepper.

Line the bottom of a baking dish (about 9½ x 7 in/24 x 17 cm) with a little of the tomato sauce and top with a couple of *lasagne* sheets. Scatter over a layer of fried vegetables, add another layer of tomato sauce and a few basil leaves, followed by some of the ricotta mixture, and a few mozzarella cubes. Continue making layers like these until you have finished the ingredients, ending with a layer of tomato sauce and mozzarella cubes.

Cover with foil and bake in the hot oven for 15 minutes. Remove the foil and continue to bake for a further 15 minutes, until golden and cooked through. Remove from the oven, leave to rest for 5 minutes, then serve.

CANNELLONI CON LE BIETOLE

Cannelloni Filled with Chard

Traditionally, *cannelloni* are filled with meat or, for a veggie option, the classic spinach and ricotta combination. I love the taste of Swiss chard and have combined it here with a little potato and cheese for a different but delicious filling. I've used colorful rainbow chard, but you can also use regular green chard.

Serves 4

1 quantity of Basic Tomato Sauce (see page 162)

2 tablespoons (1 oz/30 g) butter

½ small onion, very finely chopped

1 lb (450 g) rainbow chard, finely sliced, including stalks

1 potato (about 5 oz/150 g), peeled and grated

3 tablespoons grated Parmesan, plus extra for topping

⅓ cup (1 oz/30 g) grated provolone cheese

14 dried *cannelloni* pasta tubes

sea salt and freshly ground black pepper

Make the tomato sauce according to the recipe on page 162.

Preheat the oven to 400°F (200°C).

Melt the butter in a large frying pan over medium heat, then add the onion, and sweat for a couple of minutes. Stir in the chard and season with salt and pepper. Reduce the heat, cover, and cook for about 10 minutes, until the chard is tender—the stalk should be *al dente*. Stir in the grated potato and cook for a further 7 minutes. Remove from the heat and stir in the grated Parmesan and provolone. Fill the *cannelloni* pasta tubes with this mixture.

Line a baking dish (about 11 x 9 in/28 x 22 cm) with some of the tomato sauce, lay the filled *cannelloni* tubes on top, and pour over the remaining tomato sauce. Sprinkle with some grated Parmesan, cover with foil, and bake in the hot oven for 20 minutes.

Remove the foil and bake for a further 15 minutes.

CANNELLONI RIPIENI CON PROSCIUTTO COTTO E RICOTTA

Italian Cooked Ham and Ricotta Cannelloni

This simple *cannelloni* dish is especially loved by kids, with a light but tasty filling of cooked ham and ricotta. Ensure you use Italian cooked ham—*prosciutto cotto*—which is readily available in Italian delis; it really does have a unique taste and will enhance this dish. If you prefer, you could substitute mortadella. Allow three to four *cannelloni* per person for a main meal, served alongside a mixed salad. If serving as an appetizer (as Italians traditionally do), then two per person should suffice.

Serves 3–4

1 cup (9 oz/250 g) ricotta

6 oz (175 g) *prosciutto cotto* Italian cooked ham, finely chopped

⅔ cup (2 oz/60 g) grated Parmesan

12 dried cannelloni pasta tubes

sea salt and freshly ground black pepper

For the tomato sauce:

1 tablespoon extra-virgin olive oil

¼ onion, finely chopped

1 x 14 oz (400 g) can of chopped plum tomatoes

a few basil leaves, roughly torn

sea salt

continued overleaf

First, make the tomato sauce. Heat the olive oil in a saucepan over medium heat, add the onion, and sweat for 1 minute or so until softened. Stir in the tomatoes, some water (about a quarter of the tomato can), some salt to taste, and the basil leaves. Cover with a lid and simmer over low–medium heat for about 20 minutes.

Meanwhile, make the white sauce. Melt the butter in a small saucepan over medium heat, remove from the heat and, using a small whisk, mix in the flour very quickly to avoid lumps, then gradually add the milk, whisking well. Return to the heat and cook for 3–4 minutes, whisking all the time, until the sauce begins to thicken. Remove from the heat, season with salt and pepper, and stir in the grated Parmesan. Set aside.

Preheat the oven to 400°F (200°C).

Baked Pasta

For the white sauce:
1½ tablespoons (¾ oz/20 g) butter
3 tablespoons all-purpose flour
1¼ cups (300 ml) milk
scant ½ cup (1½ oz/40 g) grated Parmesan
sea salt and freshly ground black pepper

For the *cannelloni* filling, combine the ricotta, chopped ham, ½ cup (1¼ oz/50 g) of the grated Parmesan, and some salt and pepper. With the help of a pastry bag or a small spoon, fill the *cannelloni* tubes. Alternatively, since the filling is not runny, you could take small pieces and roll into sausage shapes to fit the tubes—much easier!

Pour the tomato sauce into a baking dish, place the filled *cannelloni* on top, then pour over the white sauce and sprinkle with the remaining Parmesan. Cover with foil and bake in the hot oven for 20 minutes.

Remove the foil and bake for a further 20 minutes, until the top is a nice golden-brown and the *cannelloni* are cooked through (test with a sharp knife or wooden skewer). Leave to rest for 5 minutes, then serve.

CANNELLONI PESCE

Fish Cannelloni

This super-simple and quick seafood pasta bake makes a delicious supper at any time, from an everyday family meal to a special occasion with friends. If you like, you can substitute the cod with hake, bream, or any other white fish you prefer. Serve with a green salad and a cool, crisp glass of Alto Adige sauvignon to enhance the delicate fish and creamy sauce.

Serve 4–6

butter for greasing, plus extra to dot

14 oz (400 g) cod, coarsely chopped

7 oz (200 g) peeled shrimp

a handful of basil leaves

zest and juice of 1 lemon

18–20 dried *cannelloni* pasta tubes

1⅔ cups (400 ml) light cream

1 teaspoon pink peppercorns

⅓ cup (1 oz/30 g) grated Parmesan

sea salt and freshly ground black pepper

Preheat the oven to 350°F (180°C) and lightly grease a large baking dish with butter.

In a food processor, combine the cod, just over half of the shrimp (4½ oz/125 g), the basil, lemon zest, and a good grinding of salt and pepper, and process until finely chopped. Using a pastry bag or a teaspoon, fill the *cannelloni* pasta tubes with this mixture and place them in the prepared baking dish.

Combine the cream, lemon juice, peppercorns, and Parmesan with the remaining shrimp and add a little salt to taste. Pour this mixture all over the *cannelloni* in the dish. Dot with small pieces of butter, cover with foil, and bake in the hot oven for 25 minutes.

Remove the foil and continue to bake for a further 5–7 minutes, until lightly golden and the *cannelloni* are cooked through.

CANNELLONI DI CARNE IN BIANCO ALLA UMBRA

Meaty Cannelloni with White Sauce

This nutritious *cannelloni* dish is popular throughout Italy, and each region tends to have its own version, like this one from Umbria. Robust and meaty, this is perfect comfort food for the whole family to enjoy.

Serves 6

3 tablespoons extra-virgin olive oil

1 small onion, very finely chopped

½ celery stalk, very finely chopped

1 small carrot, very finely chopped

needles of 1 rosemary sprig,
   very finely chopped

leaves of 1 thyme sprig, finely chopped

9 oz (250 g) ground beef

9 oz (250 g) ground pork

scant ½ cup (100 ml) white wine

1 cup (250 ml) vegetable or beef stock

about 24 dried *cannelloni* pasta tubes

½ cup (1¾ oz/50 g) grated Parmesan

For the white sauce:

3½ tablespoons (1¾ oz/50 g) butter

scant ½ cup (1¾ oz/50 g) all-purpose flour

4¼ cups (1 liter) milk

pinch of sea salt

pinch of grated nutmeg

1 cup (3½ oz/100 g) grated Parmesan

Heat the olive oil in a large saucepan over medium heat, add the onion, celery, carrot, rosemary, and thyme, and sweat for about 4 minutes, until softened. Add the beef and pork, and sauté until browned. Increase the heat, add the white wine, and allow to evaporate. Season with salt and pepper, then add the stock, reduce the heat to low, and cook for about 1 hour, until all the liquid has been absorbed.

Meanwhile, make the white sauce. Melt the butter in a small saucepan, then remove from the heat and, using a small whisk, mix in the flour very quickly to avoid lumps. Gradually add the milk, whisking well between each addition. Return to the heat and cook over medium heat for 3–4 minutes, whisking all the time, until the sauce begins to thicken. Remove from the heat, season with the salt and nutmeg, and stir in the grated Parmesan. Set aside.

Preheat the oven to 400°F (200°C).

Take the meat sauce off the heat and combine with half of the white sauce. Pour a little of the remaining white sauce into a large baking dish (about 13 x 9 in/34 x 22 cm) to line the bottom. Fill the *cannelloni* pasta tubes with the meat filling mixture, either using a pastry bag or a teaspoon. Lay the filled tubes in the baking dish, pour over the remaining white sauce, and sprinkle with the Parmesan. Cover with foil and bake in the hot oven for 20 minutes.

Remove the foil and bake for a further 15–20 minutes, until golden brown.

CONCHIGLIONI AL FORNO RIPIENI DI FUNGHI E PROSCIUTTO

Baked Pasta Shells Filled with Mushrooms and Ham

It's very common in Italy to fill this large shell-shaped pasta and bake it. This is a delicious combination of ham, mushrooms, and white sauce. For vegetarians, omit the ham and increase the quantity of mushrooms. I tend to use regular white or cremini mushrooms for this recipe.

Serves 4

about 30 *conchiglioni* pasta shells

3 tablespoons extra-virgin olive oil

5½ oz (150 g) prosciutto, very finely chopped

2 garlic cloves, minced

1 lb 10 oz (750 g) mushrooms, very finely chopped

2 tablespoons white wine

2 tablespoons chopped flat-leaf parsley

sea salt and freshly ground black pepper

For the white sauce:

3 tablespoons (1½ oz/40 g) butter

⅓ cup (1½ oz/40 g) all-purpose flour

generous 2 cups (500 ml) milk

pinch of sea salt

pinch of grated nutmeg

1½ cups (5½ oz/150 g) grated Parmesan

Bring a large saucepan of salted water to a boil and cook the *conchiglioni* until *al dente* (check the instructions on your package for cooking time). Drain the pasta, rinse under cold water, and let drain upside-down on a large plate or tray, so any excess water drains off.

Heat the olive oil in a frying pan over medium–high heat, add the prosciutto, and sauté for 1 minute. Then add the garlic and sweat for 1 minute. Stir in the mushrooms, increase the heat, add the wine, and sauté for 5–7 minutes, until the mushrooms are cooked. Remove from the heat, season with salt and pepper, then stir in the parsley and let cool slightly.

Preheat the oven to 400°F (200°C).

Make the white sauce: melt the butter in a small saucepan, then remove from the heat and, using a small whisk, mix in the flour very quickly to avoid lumps. Gradually add the milk, whisking well between each addition. Return to the heat and cook over medium heat for 3–4 minutes, whisking all the time, until the sauce begins to thicken. Remove from the heat, season with salt and nutmeg, and stir in half of the grated Parmesan.

Combine a ladleful of the white sauce with the mushroom mixture and mix well. Line the bottom of a large baking dish (about 13 x 9 in/ 34 x 22 cm) with about half of the white sauce. Fill the pasta shells with the mushroom mixture and arrange them in the dish on top of the sauce. Pour over the remaining white sauce and sprinkle with the remaining grated Parmesan. Bake in the hot oven for 20 minutes, until golden and bubbly.

PACCHERI ALLA SORRENTINA

Baked Paccheri with Tomato and Mozzarella

Alla Sorrentina is a classic way of baking pasta or gnocchi in the Campania region of southern Italy, using the local ingredients of tomatoes and *bufala* mozzarella. During summer months when tomatoes are at their best, these dishes would always be made with fresh as opposed to canned tomatoes.

Serves 4–6

1 quantity of Basic Tomato Sauce
  (see page 162)

1 lb 2 oz (500 g) *paccheri* pasta

7 oz (200 g) *mozzarella di bufala*, drained and
  coarsely chopped

1 cup (3½ oz/100 g) grated Parmesan

sea salt

Make the tomato sauce according to the recipe on page 162.

Preheat the oven to 400°F (200°C).

Bring a large saucepan of salted water to a boil and cook the *paccheri* until *al dente* (check the instructions on your package for cooking time).

Drain the pasta well and combine with most of the tomato sauce, reserving a little sauce for the topping. Mix in half of the mozzarella and half of the Parmesan and transfer the mixture to a baking dish (about 11 x 7 in/28 x 18 cm). Top with the reserved tomato sauce, scatter over the remaining mozzarella, and sprinkle with the remaining Parmesan.

Bake in the hot oven for 15 minutes, until the top is crusty and golden-brown.

SPIRALI AL FORNO IN BIANCO

Baked Spirali with Peas and Zucchini

This mac 'n' cheese-style dish with creamy, nutritious ricotta is a perfect midweek meal. With the addition of peas and zucchini, it's also an ideal veggie main.

Serves 4

butter, for greasing

sea salt, for the pasta cooking water

12 oz (350 g) *spirali* pasta

1 tablespoon extra-virgin olive oil

1 garlic clove, left whole

9 oz (250 g) zucchini,
    finely chopped

1⅓ cups (7 oz/200 g) frozen peas

½ handful of basil leaves

scant ½ cup (1½ oz/40 g) grated Parmesan

For the white sauce:

3 tablespoons (1½ oz/40 g) butter

⅓ cup (1½ oz/40 g) all-purpose flour

generous 2 cups (500 ml) milk

1 cup (9 oz/250 g) ricotta

sea salt and freshly ground black pepper

First, make the white sauce: melt the butter in a small saucepan, then remove from the heat and, using a small whisk, mix in the flour very quickly to avoid lumps. Gradually add the milk, whisking well between each addition. Return to the heat and cook over medium heat for 3–4 minutes, whisking all the time, until the sauce begins to thicken. Stir in the ricotta and continue to whisk for about 30 seconds on the heat, then remove from the heat, season with salt and pepper and set aside.

Preheat the oven to 400°F (200°C). Lightly butter a deep baking dish (about 7 x 6 in/18 x 16 cm).

Bring a large saucepan of salted water to a boil and cook the *spirali* pasta until *al dente* (check the instructions on your package for cooking time).

Meanwhile, heat the olive oil in a frying pan over medium heat, add the garlic, and sweat for 1 minute, then increase the heat to medium-high, add the zucchini, and sauté for about 4 minutes until golden. Stir in the peas and continue to cook for 1 minute, until the peas are tender. Stir in the basil leaves, then remove from the heat and set aside.

Drain the pasta well, combine it with the white sauce and vegetable mixture, and transfer to the baking dish. Sprinkle with grated Parmesan and bake in the hot oven for about 20 minutes, until golden and crispy on top.

RIGATONI AL FORNO CON POLPETTINE

Baked Rigatoni with Meatballs

Whenever we had a baked pasta dish at home in Italy, *polpettine* would nearly always feature in it. My sisters would patiently make each meatball; I would be spying on them until the moment the *polpettine* came out of the pan and I would run into the kitchen and steal a few! I wasn't very popular, but the hot *polpettine* were delicious. Together with a tomato sauce and oozing mozzarella, this baked pasta dish is fit for a king!

Serves 4

1 quantity of Basic Tomato Sauce
  (see page 162)

14 oz (400 g) *rigatoni* pasta

10½ oz (300 g) mozzarella, coarsely chopped

½ cup (1¾ oz/50 g) grated Parmesan

For the meatballs:

5½ oz (150 g) ground beef

5½ oz (150 g) ground pork

3 oz (85 g) stale bread, crusts removed,
  softened in a little milk, then drained

1 small garlic clove, minced

1 tablespoon finely chopped flat-leaf parsley

⅓ cup (1 oz/30 g) grated Parmesan

1 egg

sea salt and freshly ground black pepper

flour, for dusting

vegetable oil, for deep-frying

Make the tomato sauce according to the recipe on page 162, cooking it for 40 minutes in total to make the sauce denser. Remove from the heat, let cool a little, then blend until smooth in a food processor.

Meanwhile, make the meatballs. In a large bowl, combine the ground beef and pork, bread, garlic, parsley, grated Parmesan, and egg with some salt and pepper. Shape the mixture into small balls, approximately the size of walnuts, or smaller if you prefer, and dust them with flour.

Heat enough vegetable oil for deep-frying in a deep heavy pan over medium heat to 350°F (180°C), or until a cube of bread browns in 30 seconds. Fry the meatballs, in batches, for about 5 minutes until golden. Remove with a slotted spoon and drain on paper towels.

Preheat the oven to 400°F (200°C).

Bring a large saucepan of salted water to a boil and cook the *rigatoni* until *al dente* (check the instructions on your package for cooking time).

Drain and combine the pasta with most of the tomato sauce, reserving a little sauce for the topping.

Transfer the tomato-pasta mixture to a baking dish (about 8 in/20 cm square) and mix in the mozzarella, half of the Parmesan, and the meatballs, taking care not to break them. Pour over the reserved tomato sauce and sprinkle with the remaining Parmesan. Cover with foil and bake in the hot oven for 20 minutes.

Remove the foil and bake for a further 10 minutes.

TIMBALLO DI CANDELE CON MELANZANE

Baked Pasta Ring with Eggplants

This rustic pasta bake is made in a traditional ring-shaped cake pan, of the kind used to make sweet cakes. It takes a little time to make, but once you have all the ingredients, it's simple to assemble and looks very impressive. And it's delicious too! It uses *candele* or *ziti lunghi* pasta, available in Italian delis. Once cooked, the 20 in (50 cm) long pasta tubes go around the cake pan perfectly and look lovely when sliced.

Serves 6

1 quantity of Basic Tomato Sauce
  (see page 162)

butter, for greasing

breadcrumbs, for lining the pan

2 tablespoons extra-virgin olive oil, or as
  needed

3 eggplants (about 1 lb 14 oz/850 g), partially
  peeled to create a striped effect, and sliced
  lengthwise into ¼ in (5 mm) slices

11½ oz (325 g) *candele* or *ziti lunghi* pasta

1 cup (3½ oz/100 g) grated Parmesan

a handful of basil leaves

First, prepare the Tomato Sauce as on page 162.

Preheat the oven to 350°F (180°C). Grease a ring-shaped cake pan (like a savarin mold or bundt pan) with butter and line with breadcrumbs.

Heat a large frying pan over medium heat. Brush a little olive oil over both sides of each eggplant slice and fry the slices for 2–3 minutes on each side until golden-brown. Do this in batches, being careful not to use too much olive oil, since eggplants absorb oil very easily and you don't want them to be greasy.

Bring a large saucepan of salted water to a boil and cook the pasta, carefully pushing them into the boiling water, until *al dente* (check the instructions on your package for cooking time). Drain and mix with a little of the tomato sauce and a handful of grated Parmesan, taking care not to break the pasta.

To assemble the *timballo*: place the eggplant slices around all sides of the prepared pan until it is completely lined. You should have 5–6 slices left over—set these aside. Next, add a layer of *candele* pasta, carefully winding it around the pan. Add a layer of tomato sauce, then scatter over a few basil leaves and a layer of grated Parmesan. Continue making layers of pasta, tomato sauce, basil leaves, and grated Parmesan until you have used all the ingredients. Top with the remaining eggplant slices. Cover with foil and bake in the hot oven for 25 minutes. Remove the foil and continue to bake for a further 20 minutes.

Remove from the oven, let rest for 5 minutes, then very carefully invert the *timballo* onto a plate (just as you would a cake). Slice and enjoy!

TORTA DI RIGATONI

Rigatoni Cake

This simple pasta bake is fun to make. Basically, you stand the cooked *rigatoni* upright in a sandwich cake pan and when it comes out of the oven it looks like a pasta cake! Simply made with tomato sauce and cheese, it is great for kids' parties, but equally good to make at any time. A loose-bottomed, springform cake pan is best for getting the pasta bake out easily.

Serves 4–6

butter, for greasing

breadcrumbs, for lining the pan

11½ oz (325 g) *rigatoni* pasta

a handful of basil leaves, finely chopped

9 oz (250 g) mozzarella, cut into small cubes

½ cup (1¾ oz/50 g) grated Parmesan

sea salt and freshly ground black pepper

For the tomato sauce:

2 tablespoons extra-virgin olive oil

1 garlic clove, left whole and squashed

2 x 14 oz (400 g) cans of chopped plum tomatoes

½ handful of basil leaves, plus extra to serve

sea salt

Preheat the oven to 350°F (180°C). Line the base and sides of an 8 in (20 cm) round, loose-bottomed, springform cake pan with parchment paper, then grease with butter and coat with breadcrumbs.

To make the tomato sauce, heat the olive oil in a saucepan over medium heat, add the garlic, and sweat for 1 minute. Add the tomatoes and basil leaves, and season with salt. Cover with a lid and cook for 25 minutes, stirring occasionally. At the end of cooking, discard the garlic.

Meanwhile, bring a large saucepan of salted water to a boil and cook the pasta until *al dente* (check the instructions on your package for cooking time). Drain well and mix with the chopped basil, half of the mozzarella, some black pepper, half of the tomato sauce, and half of the grated Parmesan. Leave to cool slightly until you can handle the pasta.

Place the *rigatoni* standing upright in the prepared pan until you have filled the entire pan. Pour over the remaining tomato sauce, scatter with the remaining mozzarella, and sprinkle with the remaining grated Parmesan. Bake in the hot oven for 25 minutes, until golden.

Remove from the oven, leave to rest for 5 minutes, then carefully remove the pan, slide onto a plate, and serve, sprinkled with basil leaves.

PEPERONI RIPIENI DI PASTA

Pasta-Filled Peppers

Filled vegetables are very common throughout Italy and started off as *cucina povera*, dishes that make the veggies go further, using whatever ingredients were available. Commonly, bell peppers are baked and then filled, and the addition of pasta makes this dish a very different and enjoyable way to eat our favorite Italian staple. When you first roast the peppers, make sure you do not overcook them—they need to be sturdy to be filled with the pasta mixture. I have used red and yellow peppers since they are sweeter, but you could use the green variety too, if you prefer.

Serves 4–6

6 mixed bell peppers (yellow and red)

10½ oz (300 g) *sedanini pasta* or *pennette* (small *penne*)

2 tablespoons extra-virgin olive oil, plus extra for drizzling

1 garlic clove, left whole and squashed

4 anchovy fillets

20 pitted olives

2 teaspoons capers

10½ oz (300 g) baby plum tomatoes, halved

10 basil leaves, roughly torn

4½ oz (125 g) mozzarella, cut into small cubes

sea salt

Preheat the oven to 425°F (220°C).

Slice the tops off the peppers and using a spoon, scoop out the seeds inside. Replace the tops on the peppers to resemble little hats. Put them into a baking dish or onto a baking sheet and roast for about 15 minutes, until the peppers soften but are not mushy.

Meanwhile, bring a large saucepan of salted water to a boil and cook the pasta until *al dente* (check the instructions on your package for cooking time).

Heat the olive oil in a saucepan over medium heat, add the garlic and anchovies, and sweat until the anchovies have melted. Add the olives, capers, tomatoes, and basil, cover the pan, and cook over medium–low heat for about 7 minutes, until the tomatoes are soft. Discard the garlic.

Drain the pasta and add it to the tomato sauce, mixing well over high heat for a minute or so to combine. Remove from the heat, then stir in the mozzarella.

Reduce the oven temperature to 400°F (200°C).

Drizzle a little extra-virgin olive oil into a baking dish. Place the peppers in the dish and fill them with the pasta mixture, covering them with their little "hats." Drizzle with a little more olive oil and bake in the oven for 20 minutes. Remove from the oven, leave to rest for a couple of minutes, then serve.

In this chapter, I have included just a few of my favorite, basic Italian sauces to go with pasta. Of course there are many more sauces, whether tomato-based, cheese-based, or with meat, fish, or vegetables. Take the basic tomato sauce, add some chili or pancetta, and you have something completely different. A pesto doesn't have to be with basil, you can make it with arugula, spinach, kale, or other ingredients. It's great to experiment and find what you like, and don't forget they can all be either stored in the fridge for a few days or in the freezer to enjoy later, when you need a speedy, satisfying meal.

I always like to have some prepared sauces handy for when I don't have time to cook from scratch. When you do have time, it's worth making batches of some of your favorite sauces to have in the freezer. So, when you are in a hurry or are too tired to cook, simply cook some pasta and defrost one of the sauces to go with it. Or go one step further and you could create a lasagne in minutes with your prepared Bolognese ragú and bechamel sauce.

SAUCES

SALSA AL POMODORO

Basic Tomato Sauce

This is the most basic Italian sauce and the most widely used to flavor pasta dishes. It's handy to make a large quantity and freeze it in batches for use at other times.

Makes about 3 cups (1 lb 8 oz/680 g)
¼ cup (60 ml) extra-virgin olive oil
1 small onion, finely chopped
2 x 14 oz (400 g) cans of chopped tomatoes
½ handful of basil leaves
sea salt

Heat the olive oil in a large saucepan over medium heat, add the onion, and cook for 2–3 minutes, until softened. Add the chopped tomatoes, along with about half a tomato can of water. Season with salt, then stir in the basil leaves, cover, and simmer gently for about 20 minutes.

Use according to your recipe. Cover and store in the refrigerator for up to 3 days or freeze on the day of making.

SALSA DI POMODORI AL FORNO

Oven-Roasted Tomato Sauce

This quick and simple oven-roasted sauce is a delicious way of cooking tomatoes to obtain maximum flavor. Serve with freshly cooked pasta.

Serves 4
1 lb 9 oz (700 g) cherry or baby plum tomatoes
4 garlic cloves, left whole and squashed slightly
1 bunch of basil, leaves torn
6 tablespoons extra-virgin olive oil
sea salt
grated Parmesan, for serving (optional)

Preheat the oven to 425°F (220°C).

Place all the ingredients in a roasting pan with a generous pinch of salt and mix well. Roast in the oven for 15–20 minutes, until the tomatoes are golden and soft.

Serve with some freshly cooked *spaghetti* or your favorite pasta shape, and sprinkle with some grated Parmesan, if desired.

RAGU BOLOGNESE

Bolognese Ragù

There are so many versions of this popular pasta sauce, which is used to make the traditional *lasagne Emiliane*. Outside Italy, it can often be made quite badly. Traditional Bolognese ragù does not require canned tomatoes—this recipe gives you a rich, intense flavor using just a little tomato paste and stock. The original recipe, hailing from the gastronomic town of Bologna, used a whole cut of meat that would be hand-cut into tiny pieces, however, ready-prepared ground meat is used today, and the combination of beef and pork gives the dish more flavor. *Tagliatelle* is the preferred pasta shape for serving with this thick meat sauce.

Serves 4

3 tablespoons extra-virgin olive oil

1 onion, finely chopped

1 celery stalk, finely chopped

1 carrot, finely chopped

7 oz (200 g) ground beef

7 oz (200 g) ground pork

¾ cup (175 ml) red wine

2 tablespoons tomato paste

1 cup (250 ml) beef or vegetable stock

Heat the olive oil in a large saucepan over medium heat, add the onion, celery, and carrot, and sweat for 7–10 minutes, until the onion has softened. Add the beef and pork, and sauté until well browned. Increase the heat, add the wine, and allow to evaporate. Dilute the tomato paste in a little of the stock and stir it into the pan until well incorporated. Pour in the remaining stock and cover the pan with a lid.

Reduce the heat to low and cook for 2 hours, checking from time to time. If necessary, add a little hot water to prevent the sauce from drying out. Use according to your recipe.

SALSA DI POMODORO E VERDURINE

Tomato and Vegetable Sauce

This pasta sauce has been a favorite in my household since our girls were very young. For babies or fussy eaters, you can also blend the sauce so little ones won't notice the veggies! It's worth making lots and freezing it in batches, so you always have a quick meal on hand. Serve with cooked *penne*, *spaghetti*, or other pasta shapes, sprinkled with some grated Parmesan, and you have a quick, delicious meal in no time.

Serves 4–6

¼ cup (60 ml) extra-virgin olive oil

½ onion, finely chopped

½ celery stalk, finely chopped

1 small carrot, finely chopped

½ zucchini, finely chopped

2 x 14 oz (400 g) cans of chopped plum tomatoes

1 store-bought vegetable stock gel pot or bouillon cube

sea salt and freshly ground black pepper

Heat the olive oil in a saucepan over medium heat, add the finely chopped vegetables, and sweat for 3–4 minutes, until softened. Stir in the chopped tomatoes, along with about half a tomato can of water, and the stock gel pot or bouillon cube. Bring to a simmer, then reduce the heat, cover, and cook for 25 minutes. Check for seasoning and add a little salt and pepper if desired.

BURRO E SALVIA

Simple Butter and Sage Sauce

This quick and easy classic condiment is typically used for meat-filled *ravioli*, however you could use it simply for dressing some cooked *spaghetti* or other favorite pasta shapes. The traditional recipe uses just butter and sage, but I like to add a little vegetable stock for extra creaminess. If you don't like the pungent flavor of sage, especially if cooking for kids, just omit the sage leaves for a simple butter sauce.

Serves 4

7 tablespoons (3½ oz/100 g) unsalted butter

8 sage leaves

6 tablespoons vegetable stock

scant ½ cup (1½ oz/40 g) grated Parmesan

Heat the butter and sage leaves together in a large frying pan over medium heat, then add the stock and Parmesan and stir to combine.

Add pasta to the sauce, coating well, and continuè to cook according to your recipe. If using filled pasta, such as *ravioli*, be careful not to break them. Serve immediately.

BECHAMEL

White Sauce

This is such a versatile sauce, which is commonly used in *lasagne* and other baked pasta dishes, such as mac 'n' cheese. It can be kept in the refrigerator for about three days, or it can be frozen. Once defrosted, gently reheat in a saucepan, stirring with a wooden spoon to avoid it burning on the bottom, until it is heated through and returns to its original glossy appearance.

Serves 4–6

3 tablespoons (1½ oz/40 g) unsalted butter
⅓ cup (1½ oz/40 g) all-purpose flour
generous 2 cups (500 ml) milk
pinch of freshly grated nutmeg (optional)
sea salt and freshly ground black pepper

In a small saucepan, melt the butter over medium heat. Remove from the heat and, using a small whisk, quickly beat in the flour (to avoid lumps), then gradually add the milk, whisking all the time. Return to the heat and cook for 3–4 minutes, whisking continously, until the sauce begins to thicken slightly.

Remove from the heat and season to taste with salt and pepper and nutmeg, if desired.

PESTO GENOVESE

Basil Pesto

Basil pesto originated in Liguria, where sweet basil grows in abundance and the gentle, light olive oil is perfect for the sauce. Although there are many ready-made varieties available to buy, basil pesto is really quick and simple to make at home. It's worth making plenty, so that you can keep it in the fridge or freezer to whip up a quick pasta dish whenever you like. *Trofie*, a small thin twisty shape from the same region, is the ideal pasta for this sauce.

There are two methods you can use to make pesto: using a traditional mortar and pestle, or a food processor or blender. It's really up to you; both methods are quick, but the mortar and pestle gives a nice crunchy texture to the pesto.

Serves 4–6

1 garlic clove, peeled

2¼ cups (1¾ oz/50 g) basil leaves

2 tablespoons pine nuts

½ cup (1¾ oz/50 g) grated Parmesan

⅓ cup (1 oz/30 g) grated pecorino

⅓ cup (80 ml) extra-virgin olive oil

sea salt

With a mortar and pestle: Pound the garlic to a paste with a pinch of sea salt. Add the basil leaves and continue to pound, adding the pine nuts and cheeses as you go. Continue pounding the mixture until you get a coarse paste, then gradually drizzle in the olive oil until well combined.

With a food processor or blender: Pulse the garlic and a pinch of salt together to a paste. Add the basil leaves and pulse briefly, then add the pine nuts and cheeses. Continue to pulse to a paste, but don't overdo it—the heat from the machine may spoil the pesto, making it bitter. Gradually add the olive oil, pulsing as you go, until well combined.

Toss the pesto through freshly cooked *trofie* or other pasta shapes. Alternatively, store in an airtight container in the refrigerator for up to a week. You can also freeze pesto—a tip is to place it in an ice-cube tray and defrost only what you need.

PESTO DI ZUCCHINI

Zucchini Pesto

Here is a different green pesto that goes perfectly with cooked *trofie*, *pennette*, *farfalle*, or *spaghetti*. If you are not using it immediately, store in the refrigerator, topped with a little extra-virgin olive oil and covered with plastic wrap.

Serves 4–6

4 tablespoons extra-virgin olive oil
9 oz (250 g) zucchini, coarsely chopped
1 heaped tablespoons pine nuts
1 heaped tablespoons blanched almonds
scant ½ cup (1¼ oz/35 g) grated pecorino
scant ½ cup (1½ oz/40 g) grated Parmesan
a handful of basil leaves
a handful of mint leaves
1 garlic clove, peeled
sea salt

Heat 1 tablespoon of the olive oil in a frying pan over medium–high heat, add the zucchini, and sauté for 4–5 minutes, until it is just beginning to color. Remove from the heat and leave to cool.

Put the cooled zucchini, along with the remaining 3 tablespoons of olive oil, into a food processor or blender. Add the rest of the ingredients and process until smooth.

INDEX

GRAZIE!

To Liz Przybylski for writing and for organizing me!

To Adriana Contaldo for testing recipes and cooking at the photoshoots.

To David Loftus for beautiful photos.

To Pip Spence for lovely food styling and sourcing gorgeous props. And to Jodie Kreft who helped on set.

To Kitty Coles for helping with food styling.

To Penny Forster-Brown for helping on the shoots (and delicious cake!).

To Emily Preece-Morrison for editing.

To my agent, Luigi Bonomi.

To my publisher, Polly Powell, commissioning editor, Stephanie Milner, and design manager, Laura Russell, plus Katie Cowan, Helen Lewis, and all at Pavilion Books.